Fat Quarter Small Quilts

Darlene Zimmerman

©2005 Darlene Zimmerman
Published by

kp books
An Imprint of F+W Publications

700 East State Street • Iola, WI 54990-0001
715-445-2214 • 888-457-2873

Our toll-free number to place an order or obtain a free catalog is
800-258-0929.

Companion Angle™, Easy Angle™, Easy Scallop™, Tri-Recs™ Tool,
OxiClean®, Thermore® by Hobbs Bonded Fibers, Roxanne's Glue
Baste-It™, Thread Heaven®, EZ® Quilting by Wrights®

Library of Congress Catalog Number: 2004113673

ISBN: 0-87349-945-X

Edited by Candy Wiza
Designed by Donna Mummery

Printed in the United States of America

Dedication

This book is dedicated to the memory of my sister, Donna (Schefus) Strobl, who will be sadly missed by her family and friends.

Acknowledgments

This book would not have been possible without the input and assistance from the following people:

- ✸ My family, for being so patient with me and for their honest opinions.
- ✸ Julie Stephani, the acquisitions editor, who does miracles with scheduling.
- ✸ Brenda Mazemke, for her suggestion and encouragement.
- ✸ Niki Gould, my editor, for all her help for the first half of the book.
- ✸ Candy Wiza, my editor, for all her help for the second half of the book.
- ✸ My daughter, Rachel, for creating the wonderful graphics for this book.
- ✸ Kris Kandler, the photographer, for making my work look beautiful.
- ✸ Donna Mummery, the book designer, for doing such a great job!
- ✸ My friend, Bonny Hartung, for opening her Quilt Haven for photography.
- ✸ My friends, Pam, Bonny and Margy, for advice and encouragement.
- ✸ Margy Manderfeld, for sharing her "Perfect Fit" binding technique for this book.
- ✸ American & Efird Inc., for supplying me with the threads for the projects.
- ✸ Hobbs Bonded Fibers and Fairfield Processing Corp., for supplying the batting for the projects.
- ✸ Chanteclaire Fabrics, RJR Fabrics and Debbie Beaves for supplying the fabrics for the projects in this book.

Table of Contents

Introduction

Small quilts.... quilts that are small in scale and size (although not miniature) are the focus for this book. Small quilts are quick to make when you need a break from a larger project, when you need a gift for someone, or have a special place to decorate. They allow you to explore colorations outside your comfort zone, try a new tool or technique, or, finally use some of the fabulous fat quarter bundles in your stash!

Small quilts also are easy to decorate with, as they are quick to hang. Insert a dowel in the sleeve on the back and they can be hung like a picture. Quickly change your décor on a whim. The small quilts can be hung on a wall, draped over a piece of furniture, laid on a flat surface like an old-fashioned doily, or used as a centerpiece on a table. Throughout the book you will see little quilts displayed in many different settings with a few well-chosen accessories. Use the decorating ideas shown to duplicate this look in your home, or as a springboard for new ideas.

The 25 projects shown are quite easy as the blocks in the quilts are simple ones. You will find complete instructions with detailed graphics to walk you through the step-by-step process and make it enjoyable. Even the quilting will be easy, as the quilts are small enough to easily maneuver under your sewing machine needle. They make great take-along projects for hand appliqué or quilting. I hope you have as much fun making these projects as I did!

General Instructions

Choosing Fabric

Choosing fabric for a project can be the most enjoyable part of the whole process. Don't be afraid of this step! Start with one fabric you really like and pull the coordinating colors from it. Or, even easier, use one of those coordinated fat quarter bundles you have purchased. Those fabrics have been selected by experts in the quilt shop, or may be part or all of a fabric collection — in which case the fabrics are designed to work together!

You can choose the same fabrics for a small quilt that you would pick for a large quilt. The scale of the design does not have to be small. Choose a large design if it looks good cut into smaller pieces. Also choose a larger print for the border or large units in the quilt such as alternate blocks. If in doubt, make up one block before cutting the whole project.

Preparation

You may choose to pre-wash your fabrics — or not. They lose some of their body when you wash them, and you may have some loss with raveling. A little spray starch or sizing can restore the body.

If you are eager to start a new project, you can simply pretest for color bleeding by spritzing a small area of the fabric with water, placing a white fabric over it, then ironing. If you get color transfer, perhaps you'd better pre-wash.

Ironing the folds out of the fabrics before cutting is a necessary step for accurate cutting.

Cutting

Accuracy is always important in the cutting process, but even more so with little quilts; there is less room for error. Also, the pieces will fit together more readily if you've taken the time to cut them accurately. Some tips for accurate cutting:

* Work in good light, daylight if possible.

* Iron the fabrics before cutting.

* Cut only two layers of fabric at a time. Any time you save in cutting more layers will be lost when the pieces don't fit accurately.

* Keep your tools from slipping — use the film or sandpaper that adheres to the backside of the tools.

* Use a sharp rotary cutter and a good mat. Mats do wear out after a time, as too many grooves get cut into them. Replace blades and mats as needed; this is not an area to cut corners (no pun intended!).

Using the Tools

Note that each of the patterns suggests various tools, but optional cutting directions also are given. The recommended tools are designed to allow you to cut even-size strips and exactly the right shape and size you need. **The tools are not interchangeable!** Use the right tool to cut the pieces. A tool tutorial is given on pages 122-127, so you can familiarize yourself with how they are properly used.

About the Cutting Tables...

Each pattern has a cutting table stating which fabric to cut into how many strips. Note the strip lengths vary; some directions are written for fat quarters, others for full width yardage. The second column (under CUT) will give you that information. The last column tells you how many pieces, what shape and what tool to use to cut them.

Sewing

Quarter-inch seams are so important! If at all possible, find a ¼" foot for your sewing machine. They are well worth the small investment.

If you have problems with the mad feed dogs chewing up your fabric, try these tricks to "tame" them:

* Insert a new needle, preferably a smaller one.

* Clean your sewing machine, particularly the fuzz under the throat plate.

* Consider switching to a single-hole throat plate (instead of the wide opening for zigzag).

* Chain-sew whenever possible.

* Begin and end with a scrap of fabric, an "engine" and "caboose."

Un-sewing

It's a fact of life, sometimes we make mistakes or the pieces don't fit properly. Fortunately, the seams on little quilts are short and the pieces small, so any un-sewing goes quickly. However, don't get hung up on perfection. Fix the areas that bother you (learn from your mistakes!) and move on to the next step.

Pressing

Remember the purpose of pressing is to make the seam/unit/block/quilt FLAT. Keep that thought in mind while pressing. I prefer to iron from the right side whenever possible. Pressing arrows are given in the diagrams. If you use these, most, if not all, of your seams will alternate.

TIP: Try this quick check to see if you are sewing an exact ¼" seam: Cut three 1½" x 3½" strips. Sew them together on the long edges. Press. The square should now measure 3½". If not, adjust your seam allowance. (Also, check that you have pressed correctly.)

Twisting the Seam

Try this neat trick whenever piecing any type of four-patch unit. It will make the center intersection lie flatter.

1. Before pressing the last seam on a four-patch, grasp the seam with both hands about an inch from the center seam. Twist in opposite directions, opening up a few threads in the seam.

2. Press one seam one direction, the other seam the opposite direction. In the center you will see a tiny four-patch appear, and the center now lays flat.

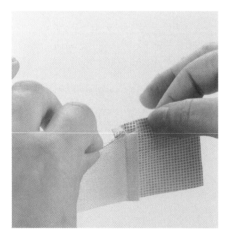

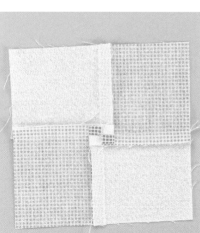

Borders

We often make this more difficult than it needs to be. Simply cut the strips designated for the borders, place them on top of the quilt, measuring through the middle of the quilt. Measure for the borders with the fabric strips themselves. Always "measure" with two strips at a time so the borders are guaranteed to be the same length! I crease the border at the proper length, and cut a bit longer for "insurance." Pin the borders to the quilt, and sew.

Mitered Borders

Occasionally, to look best, borders need to be mitered. To cut mitered borders, add the *width* of two extra borders to the length. Also, add a couple of inches for "insurance." For example: the quilt top measures 20" x 30" and you are adding 3" wide borders. For the top

and bottom of the quilt you would cut 20" + 3" + 3" + 2" (insurance) = 28". For the sides, 30" + 3" + 3" + 2" = 38".

1. Find the center of each border and the center of the corresponding edge of the quilt. Pin together in the center. Sew the borders to the quilt, stopping and backstitching ¼" from the corner of the quilt.

2. Fold the quilt on the diagonal, with right sides together, matching raw edges of the borders. The borders will extend outward.

3. Place the Companion Angle (or a ruler) on your quilt with the longest edge on the diagonal of the quilt, and a 45-degree line (or the edge of the Companion Angle) aligned with the raw edges of the borders.

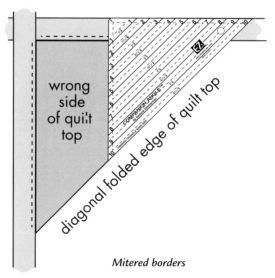

Mitered borders

4. Draw a diagonal line from the end of the stitching line to the raw edges of the border.

5. Pin the borders together along this marked line. Sew on the line, backstitching at the inside corner.

6. Check the seam on the right side. If it lies flat and there are no tucks or pleats, trim the seam to ¼". Press open, or to one side. Repeat on all four corners.

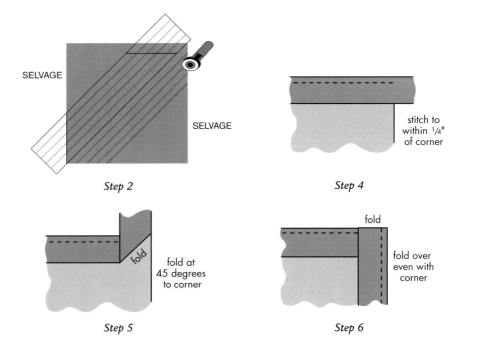

SELVAGE

SELVAGE

stitch to within ¼" of corner

Step 2

Step 4

fold

fold at 45 degrees to corner

fold

fold over even with corner

Step 5

Step 6

Batting Choices

The small quilts look (and hang) best with a lightweight flat batting. A good choice is a lightweight cotton, or Thermore by Hobbs Bonded Fibers (a lightweight polyester batting designed for garments).

Quilting

Small quilts generally don't require lots of quilting, and easily can be machine quilted. They also are ideal take-along hand quilting projects! Quilting suggestions are given with each project. Choose to quilt them as I have done, or experiment with your own technique. This is the perfect place to try that new thread or technique.

Binding

When the quilting is complete, baste a scant ¼" around the perimeter of the quilt. This will prevent the layers from shifting while the binding is being sewn on.

1. Cut the binding strips either bias or straight-of-grain, single or double. The pattern will recommend a size and type, but the final choice is up to you! For these little quilts a single-fold binding is sufficient. Bias or straight-of-grain bindings work equally well on a straight edge. You MUST use a bias binding on scalloped or curved edges.

2. To cut bias strips, align the 45-degree line on your ruler on the left edge of your fabric. Cut on the diagonal in the width chosen for the quilt.

3. Join all binding strips with diagonal seams pressed open. For a double binding, fold in half the long way, and press with wrong sides together.

4. Sew the binding to the quilt with a ¼" seam, mitering the corners. To miter, sew within a ¼" from the corner (or the width of your seam allowance). Stop and backstitch. Remove the quilt from under the presser foot, and clip the threads.

5. Fold the binding straight up and straight back down, aligning with the next edge to be sewn.

6. Begin stitching at the fold. Repeat in this manner around the quilt.

"Perfect Fit" Join

My friend, Margy, came up with this simple, but very effective technique for joining the binding ends. It's an easy technique and works for any width binding.

1. When you begin sewing the binding, start in the middle of one side and leave an 8" tail. Continue stitching the binding until you are within 10" of the beginning. Remove the quilt from under the needle.

2. On a flat surface, pull the binding ends together to meet in the middle of that 10" space. Crease both ends where they meet, but leave a ¼" space between the ends. Cut one end off at the crease, and the other end a binding's width from the crease (if this is a double binding, open it up).

3. Join the two ends with a diagonal seam pressed open.

4. Finish sewing the binding to the quilt. Trim excess batting and backing. Turn the binding to the backside, and stitch the binding down by hand with matching thread.

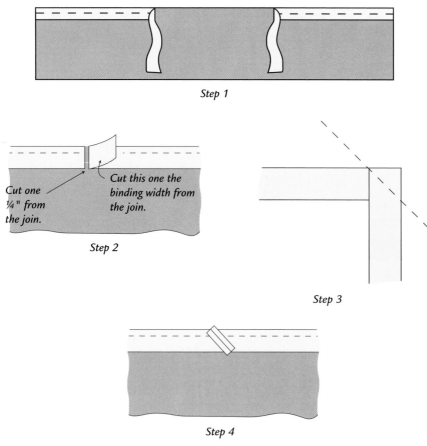

Step 1

Cut one ¼" from the join.

Cut this one the binding width from the join.

Step 2

Step 3

Step 4

Quilt Labels

Your quilts are your legacy, so sign them! An artist would sign on the front, but you may want to add more information to your quilt. A label should include the following information:

· Quilt recipient
· Quilt maker (and possibly the quilter if not yourself)
· Date of completion/ presentation
· Where it was made (city, country)
· Special occasion or story

You can purchase a fabric label to write on or create your own. Sew or appliqué the label to the quilt either before or after the quilt is completed.

Washing and Storing

With reasonable care a quilt can last for many generations. Remember to protect the quilt from light, smoke, pets, small children, high heat and humidity.

Store in a pillowcase, never in plastic, paper or against wood. Try to store flat if possible.

If washing is necessary, use one of the detergents made specifically for washing quilts. Wash the quilt in lukewarm water. If stains need to be removed, soak in a solution of OxiClean for up to three days. Do not agitate in the washing machine, but wash gently by hand. You can spin out a quilt in the washing machine to remove the excess water. Rinse in the same manner.

To dry, lay flat with a fan blowing over the quilt. Turn over and dry the backside the same way. Allow the quilt to dry thoroughly before storing. With loving care, your quilts can become treasured heirlooms for generations to come.

Freezer Paper Appliqué

The patterns given in the book are reversed for tracing purposes. Trace the shapes on the dull side of the freezer paper.

Note: You can reuse the freezer paper shapes several times.

1. Cut out the shapes on the marked lines. Iron the shape to the wrong side of the fabric chosen for the appliqué, leaving at least ¾" between the shapes. Cut out the shapes adding a scant ¼" seam allowance. Clip any inside curves.

2. With a 1:1 liquid starch and water mixture and a cotton swab, wet the seam allowance of the appliqué piece. Using the tip of the iron, press the seam allowance over the edge of the freezer paper. Once the edge is well pressed, you can remove the freezer paper and iron from the top side.

3. Baste in place on the background square either with needle and thread or Roxanne's Glue Baste-It.

4. Appliqué down by hand with matching thread or use a tiny zigzag stitch on your sewing machine. Another option would be to use black thread (machine) or black floss (hand) and a buttonhole stitch. For hand appliqué, silk thread in a light cream color works best for most fabrics. The thread "melts" into the fabrics, making your stitches nearly invisible.

Fusible Appliqué

1. Trace the reversed pattern on the paper side of the fusible web. Leave a bit of space between each appliqué pattern.

2. Cut out, leaving a small excess of paper around the appliqué. Iron to the wrong side of the fabrics chosen for the appliqués.

3. Cut out on the marked line. Peel off the backing paper. Position, and fuse in place following the manufacturer's directions.

4. Hand or machine buttonhole stitch around the shapes with matching or invisible thread.

Cut out center

TIPS

• For an appliqué that is less stiff, cut out the center of the shape on the fusible web piece. The center is then free and only the edges are fused.

• Thread Heaven, a product similar to beeswax, helps prevent silk thread from tangling.

Little Bo-Peep

Finished size: 18½" square
Block size: 3"

The inspiration for this quilt came from a darling, vintage, tinted-linen child's bib. I copied the pattern, used color crayons for the "tinting," added embroidery accents, and framed it with a border of flowers. Now the charming picture of Little Bo-Peep can be enjoyed all the time!

Fabric Requirements
⅝ yd. vintage white
4 fat quarters of assorted prints
Fat quarter green print
⅔ yd. backing

Suggested Tool
Tri-Recs
Note: There is no substitute for the Tri-Recs tools.

Additional Supplies
Basic sewing supplies
Blue washout pen
Crayons
Embroidery floss: pink, green, black, blue and gold
Thread to match fabric
23" x 23" batting

Cutting Directions

FABRIC	CUT	TO YIELD
Vintage white	1—11" x 40" strip	1—11" square
	3—2" x 40" strips	64 *pairs* of Recs* triangles
From *each* of the four fat quarter prints	2—2" x 20" strips	16 Tri triangles
Green print	3—1" x 20" strips	12—1" x 3½" sashes
	2—1" x 20" strips	2—1" x 10½" horizontal inner borders
	2—1" x 20" strips	2—1" x 17½" vertical inner borders
	4—1" x 20" strips	Outer border
	5—1¼" x 20" strips	Binding

Note: Cut the Recs triangles with the strip folded in half, cutting pairs.

Sew exact ¼" seams throughout. Place fabrics right sides together for sewing, unless otherwise noted.

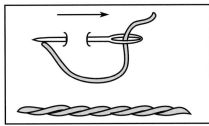

Outline Stitch

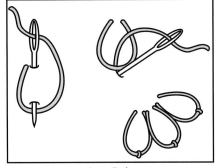

Lazy Daisy

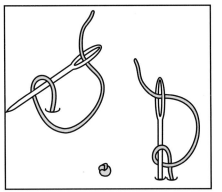

French Knot

Satin Stitch

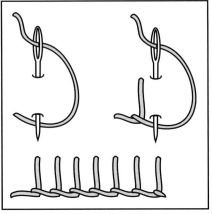

Buttonhole Stitch

Little Bo-Peep Block

1. Fold and lightly crease the 11" white square in half from both directions. Use the creases to center the Little Bo-Peep design (from page 19). Trace with the blue washout pen.

2. Color in the dress, bonnet, sheep, hair and shepherd's crook with the side of clean crayons.

3. Embroider the lines with an outline stitch and two strands of floss. Use a lazy daisy stitch for the leaves on the bonnet and the shepherd's crook, and French knots for the flowers. Satin stitch the sheep's eyes, and use a straight stitch for the grass.

4. Soak the block in cold water to remove the markings. Let dry flat.

5. Iron with the colored side down on a fluffy towel (to avoid flattening the embroidery). **Trim the block evenly to 10½" square.**

Assemble the Flower Blocks (Make 16)

Refer to page 122 for detailed instructions on sewing Tri-Recs units.

1. Sew a white Recs triangle to the right side of the print Tri triangle. Press toward the white triangle.

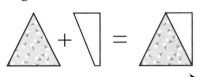

Make 64

2. Sew a white Recs triangle to the left side of the unit from Step 1. Press toward the white triangle. Repeat Steps 1 and 2 to make a total of 64 Tri-Recs units. At this point the unit should measure 2" square.

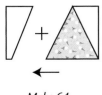

Make 64

3. Sew two matching Tri-Recs units together as shown. Repeat for the remainder of the Tri-Recs units. Press.

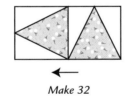

Make 32

4. Sew together two matching units from Step 3. Twist the seam where it intersects to open it. Press. Refer to page 10 for more instructions on this technique. Make 16 flower blocks. At this point the blocks should measure 3½" square.

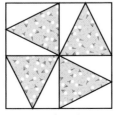

Make 16

Assemble the Quilt

1. Sew together three flower blocks and two 1" x 3½" green sashing strips. Press toward the sashing strips. Make two of these units.

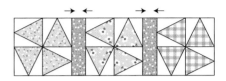

2. Sew green 1" x 10½" inner borders to one side of the units from Step 1. Press toward the inner border. Sew the borders with flower blocks to the top and bottom of the embroidered picture. Press toward the inner borders.

3. Sew the 1" x 17½" green vertical borders to the side edges of the quilt. Press toward the borders. Sew four green sashes and five blocks together as in Step 1. Make two of these flower borders. Press, and sew the flower borders to the sides of the quilt. Press toward the green sashings.

Borders

Refer to page 10 for detailed instructions on adding borders. Measure, cut and sew 1" wide green borders to the top and bottom of the quilt. Press toward the borders. Repeat this procedure for the sides of the quilt.

Quilting Suggestions

To prepare the quilt for quilting, layer the backing (which has been cut at least 4" larger than the quilt top) wrong side up, followed by the batting (again, cut larger than the quilt top) and last, the quilt top, right-side up. Thread baste or pin baste in a 4" grid across the quilt. Quilt as desired.

The quilt shown was crosshatched by hand around the embroidered picture. I quilted in the ditch around the motifs in the picture, around each of the blocks and through the middle of the flowers.

Binding

Refer to page 11 for detailed instructions on adding binding.

1. Before binding, hand baste a scant ¼" from the edge of the quilt. This will prevent the layers from shifting while the binding is being sewn on.

2. Join the ends of the binding with diagonal seams pressed open.

3. Sew to the quilt with a ¼" seam. Trim excess batting and backing.

4. Turn the binding to the backside. Turn the binding under ¼", and stitch down by hand with matching thread.

5. Sign and date your little quilt!

Gingham Flowers

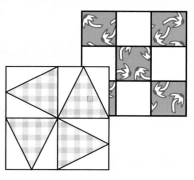

Finished size: 25½" x 33½"
Block size: 3"

There is something so delightful about gingham, even though woven or printed gingham fabrics have been around for more than 200 years. In this quilt, different colors of gingham "flowers" have been framed with a latticework of green print. The lattice is created with simple nine-patch blocks, and the two different blocks are set with sashing and cornerstones. What looks like a difficult quilt is indeed quite simple to make.

Fabric Requirements
¾ yd. vintage white
Fat quarters pink, blue, yellow and lavender gingham (or any four fabrics)
⅞ yd. green print
⅞ yd. backing

Suggested Tool
Tri-Recs
Note: There is no substitute for the Tri-Recs tools.

Additional Supplies
Basic sewing supplies
Thread to match fabric
30" x 38" batting

Cutting Directions for Flower Blocks

FABRIC	CUT	TO YIELD
Vintage white	4—2" x 40" strips	68 pairs of Recs* triangles
From *three* gingham fat quarters	2—2" x 20" strips	16 Tri triangles
From *one* gingham fat quarter	2—2" x 20" strips	20 Tri triangles

*Note: When cutting with the Recs tool, fold the strip in half and cut pairs. Don't forget to trim off the "magic angle." Refer to page 122 for detailed instructions on using the Tri-Recs tools.

Sew exact ¼" seams throughout. Place fabrics right sides together for sewing, unless otherwise noted.

Assemble the Flower Blocks (Make 17)

1. Open up the pairs of Recs triangles and place them on either side of the Tri triangles as shown (A). Sew a Recs triangle to the right side of the Tri triangle, fitting the "magic angle" into the corner (B). Press the seam toward the Recs triangle.

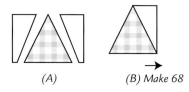

(A)   *(B) Make 68*

2. Sew a Recs triangle to the left side of the Tri-Recs units from Step 1. Press toward the triangle just added. At this point the unit should measure 2" square.

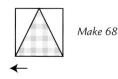

Make 68

3. Sew the Tri-Recs units from Step 2 together in matching pairs as shown. Press.

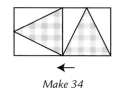

Make 34

4. Sew matching pairs together to make flower blocks, matching and pinning at the intersection. Twist the seam where it intersects to open it. Press. Refer to page 10 for more instruction on this technique. At this point the flower blocks should measure 3½".

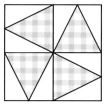

Make 17

Cutting Directions for Nine-Patch Blocks and Sashing

FABRIC	CUT	TO YIELD
Vintage white	4—1½" x 40" strips	Strip sets
	6—1½" x 40" strips	58—1½" x 3½" sashes
Green print	5—1½" x 40" strips	Strip sets
	1—1½" x 40" strip	24—1½" squares (cornerstones)

Assemble the Nine-Patch Blocks (Make 18)

1. Sew together two strip sets of green, white, green. Press toward the green strips. At this point the strip sets should measure 3½" wide. Cut into 36 units 1½" wide.

2. Sew together one strip set of white, green, white. Press toward the green strip. Cut into 18 units 1½" wide.

3. Sew together two units from Step 1 and one unit from Step 2 to make a nine-patch block. Press. Make 18 blocks. At this point the blocks should measure 3½".

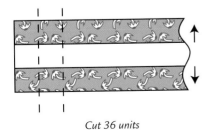

Cut 36 units

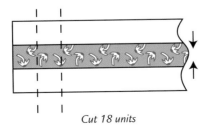

Cut 18 units

Make 18 blocks

Assemble the Quilt

1. Sew four white 1½" x 3½" sashing strips, three nine-patch blocks and two flower blocks together to make a row. Press toward the sashing strips. Make four rows.

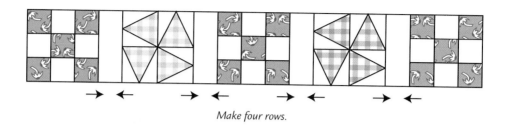

Make four rows.

2. Sew four white 1½" x 3½" sashing strips, two nine-patch blocks and three flower blocks together to make a row. Press toward the sashing strips. Make three rows.

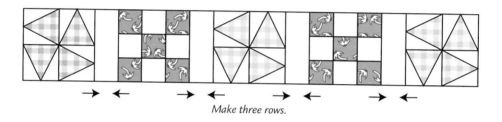

Make three rows.

3. Sew five white 1½" x 3½" sashes and four green cornerstones together to make a horizontal sashing row. Press toward the sashing strips. Make six rows.

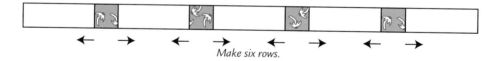

Make six rows.

4. Sew the Step 1, Step 2 and Step 3 rows together according to the photo on page 27. Press the seams toward the horizontal sashing rows.

Cutting Directions for Borders and Binding

FABRIC	CUT	TO YIELD
Green print	7—1½" x 40" strips	Inner and outer borders
	4—2" strips	Binding
From *each* gingham fat quarter	2—1½" x 20" strips	Strip sets

Borders

Refer to page 10 for detailed instructions on adding borders.

1. Measure, cut and sew a 1½" green border to the top and bottom of the quilt. Press toward the border.

2. In the same manner, measure, cut and sew a 1½" green border to the sides of the quilt. Press toward the border.

3. Sew the gingham strips together in this order: pink, blue, lavender and yellow. Press the seams all in one direction. Make two strip sets. Cut the strip sets into 26 units 1½" wide.

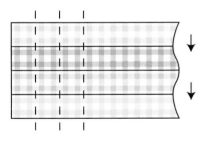

4. Join six units from Step 3 to make the top border. Remove the last three squares. The border should begin and end with a pink square. Press. Make a second border just like this for the bottom of the quilt. Sew pieced borders to the top and bottom of the quilt. Press toward the green border.

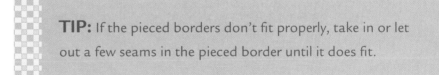

5. Starting with the squares removed from the top and bottom borders, piece together eight units, including the partial unit from Step 4. The borders should have a yellow square on one end and a blue square on the other. Press seams all one direction. Make two. Sew borders to the sides of the quilt. Press toward the green border.

6. In the same manner as in Step 1 and 2, measure, cut and sew the green outer borders to the quilt. Press toward the borders just added.

TIP: If the pieced borders don't fit properly, take in or let out a few seams in the pieced border until it does fit.

Quilting Suggestions

To prepare the quilt for quilting, layer the backing (which has been cut at least 4" larger than the quilt top) wrong side up, followed by the batting (again, cut larger than the quilt top) and last, the quilt top, right-side up. Thread or pin baste in a 4" grid across the quilt. Quilt as desired.

The quilt shown was machine meandered in all the white areas. Straight lines, following the seam lines in the pieced borders, were hand quilted in the three borders.

Binding

Refer to page 11 for detailed instructions on binding a quilt.

1. Before binding, hand baste a scant ¼" from the edge of the quilt. This will prevent the layers from shifting while the binding is being sewn on.

2. Join the binding ends with diagonal seams pressed open.

3. Press the binding in half lengthwise with wrong sides together.

4. Sew to the quilt with a ¼" seam, mitering the corners.

5. Turn the binding to the backside and stitch down by hand with matching thread.

6. Sign and date your Gingham Flowers quilt!

Baskets and Posies

Finished size: 25" x 31" including prairie points
Block size: 4"

The unusual setting displays the simple little basket blocks in an attractive way. The appliquéd flowers and prairie points accent this charming little quilt. This project can be hand or machine appliquéd.

Fabric Requirements

⅝ yd. vintage white
½ yd. green print
2" x 20" yellow solid
6 fat quarters of assorted prints
⅞ yd. backing

Suggested Tools

Easy Angle
Companion Angle

Additional Supplies

Basic sewing supplies
Thread to match fabric
Freezer paper or fusible web
Liquid starch
Off-white silk thread
Glue Baste-It
Thread Heaven
29" x 35" batting

Note: If not using the Easy Angle, cut 3⅞", 2⅞", and 1⅞" squares, respectively. Cut once on the diagonal to make triangles.

If not using the Companion Angle, cut two 8¼" squares. Cut twice on the diagonal to yield eight triangles.

Cutting Directions for Basket Blocks

FABRIC	CUT	TO YIELD
Vintage white	1—3½" x 40" strip	18 Easy Angle triangles
	3—2½" x 40" strips	18 Easy Angle triangles
		36—1½" x 2½" rectangles
From *each* fat quarter	1—3½" x 20" strip	3—3½" Easy Angle triangles
	1—1½" x 20" strip	6—1½" Easy Angle triangles
		3 handles

Sew exact ¼" seams throughout. Place fabrics right sides together for sewing, unless otherwise noted.

Assemble the Basket Blocks (Make 18)

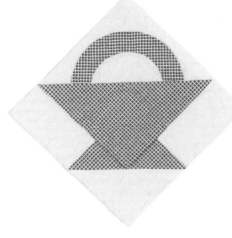

Refer to page 13 for detailed instructions on freezer paper and fusible appliqué.

1. Trace the handle template (page 32) onto freezer paper. Cut out several freezer paper templates (you can reuse them several times). Iron the templates to the wrong side of the fabric for the baskets. Cut out, adding a scant ¼" seam allowance. Clip the inside curve at regular intervals. Using a cotton swab and diluted 1:1 liquid starch, wet the seam allowance. Iron the seam allowance over the freezer paper, leaving the ends of the handle free. Remove the freezer paper template.

2. With hand or machine, appliqué the handles in place on the white 3½" triangles. Sew the white triangles with appliquéd handles to the large print triangle. Press the seam allowance toward the basket. Make 18.

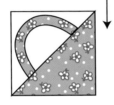

Make 18

3. Sew the small print triangles to the ends of the white rectangles as shown. Press toward the triangles. Make 18 pairs.

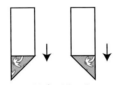

Make 18 pairs

4. Sew the units from Step 3 to the Step 2 basket. Press the seams toward the basket. Add the 2½" white triangle to the bottom of the basket. At this point the basket block should measure 4½". Make 18 blocks.

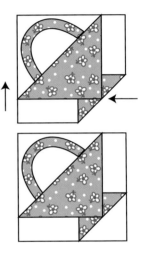

Make 18

Cutting Directions for Quilt Assembly

FABRIC	CUT	TO YIELD
Vintage white	2—4½" x 40" strips	2—4½" x 12½" rectangles
		2—4½" x 8½" rectangles
Green print	1—10" x 40" strip	2—10" squares, cut once on the diagonal to yield four triangles
	1—4" x 40" strip	6 Companion Angle triangles
Fat quarter prints	50—3" squares	Prairie points

Assemble the Quilt

1. Sew four baskets together with the handles facing in. Press. Sew a white 4½" x 8½" rectangle to opposite sides of the basket blocks. Sew a pair of baskets to both ends of the basket/rectangle unit. Press.

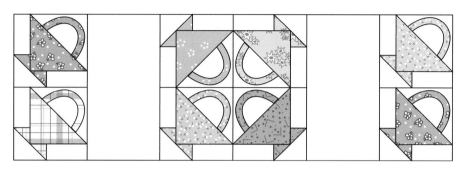

2. Sew three baskets together in a row. Make two. Press.

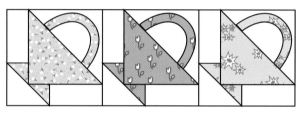

Make two

3. Sew a basket block to both ends of the 4½"x 12½" white rectangle. Make two. Press.

Make two

4. Using the large and small green triangles, and the units from Steps 1, 2, and 3, assemble the quilt according to the photo on page 33. Press. Note the outside triangles are larger than needed.

Appliqué the Flowers

1. Trace the flower, center and leaf patterns from page 32 onto freezer paper. Cut out on the marked line.

2. Iron the templates to the wrong side of the fabrics for the flowers. Cut out, adding a scant ¼" seam allowance, and snipping into the "V's" on the flower.

3. Using a cotton swab and diluted 1:1 liquid starch, wet the seam allowance. Iron the edges of the fabric around the templates. Remove the templates. Baste or glue-baste the flowers and leaves in place.

4. Machine or hand appliqué the leaf, flower and center onto the white rectangles, referring to the photo on page 33 for placement and orientation.

Prairie Point Edging

1. Trim the edges of the quilt square, leaving at least ¼" or more from the corners of the blocks.

2. Fold the 3" print squares in half once on the diagonal, press. Fold again on the diagonal and press.

3. Tuck one prairie point inside the other, overlapping at least ¼". You will need 11 prairie points each for the top and bottom of the quilt, and 14 for each side of the quilt.

4. Baste together a scant ¼" from the bottom of the prairie points. Adjust the prairie points as needed to fit the quilt top exactly. They need to come to the corner as shown.

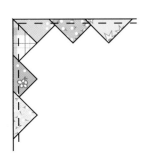

5. Sew the prairie points to the quilt with a ¼" seam. At this time the prairie points will be folded to the interior of the quilt.

Quilting Suggestions

To prepare the quilt for quilting, layer the backing (which has been cut at least 4" larger than the quilt top) wrong side up, followed by the batting (again, cut larger than the quilt top) and last, the quilt top, right-side up. Thread baste or pin baste in a 4" grid across the quilt. Quilt as desired. Move the prairie points out of the way when quilting, **leaving 1" from the edge unquilted.**

The quilt shown was machine meandered in the white areas around the baskets. The green outer triangles were hand quilted in a 1" grid pattern.

Finish the Quilt

1. Trim the batting ¼" shorter than the quilt top. Trim the back of the quilt even with the raw edge of the top of the quilt. Turn the prairie points to the outside of the quilt.

2. Turn the backing under ¼" and slip stitch in place over the quilt front.

3. Finish quilting close to the edge.

4. Sign and date your sweet, little baskets quilt!

Twist and Shout!

Finished size: 21¼" x 25¼"
Block size: 2¾"

Pinwheel, Whirligig and Waterwheel are all names for the block used in this quilt. It's an interesting block, but we tend to avoid it because it involves using templates. I've eliminated the templates by strip piecing, then cutting triangles from the strips. There is a bit of waste with this method, but since the pieces are so small, it is worth the time it saves! You'll find this to be a quick and easy quilt.

Fabric Requirements

1 yd. vintage white
6 fat quarters of assorted prints
Fat quarter red check (binding)
¾ yd. backing

Additional Supplies

Basic sewing supplies
Thread to match fabric
26" x 29" batting

Cutting Directions

FABRIC	CUT	TO YIELD
Vintage white	10—1¾" x 40" strips	30—1¾" x 13" strips for blocks
	5—1¼" x 40" strips	49—1¼" x 3¼" sashes
	6—1¼" x 40" strips	Inside and outside borders
From *each* of six fat quarter prints	5—1¾" x 20" strips	5—1¾" x 13" strips for blocks
	1—1¼" x 20"	4—1¼" x 3¼" border segments
		5—1¼" squares
Red check	2" bias strips	Binding

Sew exact ¼" seams throughout. Place fabrics right sides together for sewing, unless otherwise noted.

Block Assembly
(Make 30)

1. Sew 1¾" x 13" white and print strips together (A). Press the seam toward the darkest fabric. Cut each strip set into four 3" squares (A), then cut each square once on the diagonal (B). Discard the triangles that are mostly white (C).

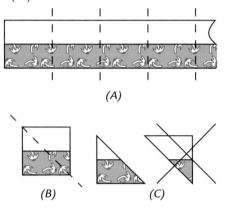

(A)

(B) (C)

2. Sew four matching triangles together in pairs as shown (A). Press. Sew the pairs together. Twist the seam where it intersects to open it. Press. Refer to page 10 for more instruction on this technique. **Trim to 3¼" square.** Repeat to make 30 blocks (B).

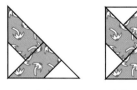

(A) (B) Make 30

TIP: If the pieced borders don't fit exactly, you can take in or let out a few seams interspersed throughout the border.

Assemble the Quilt

1. Join five blocks in a row with four white sashing strips. Press toward the sashing strips. Make six rows.

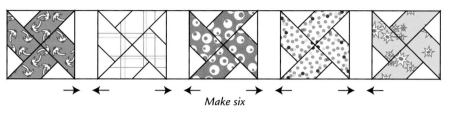

Make six

2. Sew together five horizontal sashing rows with five white sashing strips and four print squares. Press toward the sashing strips.

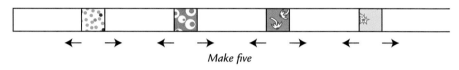

Make five

3. Join the block rows and the sashing rows, matching and pinning at each seam intersection. Press the rows toward the sashings.

Borders

Refer to page 10 for detailed instructions on adding borders.

1. Measure the quilt top through the middle of the quilt. Take this measurement and trim two white borders the width of the quilt. Sew to the quilt. Press toward the borders.

2. Measure the length of the quilt. Cut two white borders the length of the quilt. Sew to the quilt. Press toward the borders.

3. Piece together five print border segments alternated with six print squares to make a top border. Press.

4. Piece a similar border for the bottom of the quilt. Sew to the top and bottom of the quilt. Press toward the white border.

5. Piece together six border segments alternated with nine squares for the sides of the quilt (two segments at each end). Make two pieced borders. Sew to the quilt, pressing the seams toward the white border.

6. Measure, cut and sew the last white border to the top and bottom of the quilt. Measure, cut and sew the sides in the same manner. Press the seams toward the last border.

Quilting Suggestions

To prepare the quilt for quilting, layer the backing (which has been cut at least 4" larger than the quilt top) wrong side up, followed by the batting (again, cut larger than the quilt top) and last, the quilt top, right-side up. Thread or pin baste in a 4" grid across the quilt. Quilt as desired.

The quilt shown was machine quilted in the ditch along the horizontal and vertical sashes and cornerstones, as well as on each side of the borders. An "X" was hand stitched through the middle of the blocks.

Binding

Refer to page 11 for detailed instructions on binding a quilt.

1. Before binding, hand baste a scant ¼" from the edge of the quilt to prevent the layers from shifting.

2. Join the binding strips with diagonal seams pressed open. Press the binding in half lengthwise with wrong sides together.

3. Sew the binding to the quilt with a ¼" seam allowance. Trim the excess batting and backing.

4. Turn the binding to the backside and stitch down by hand with matching thread.

5. Sign and date your little quilt.

Star Flowers

Finished size: 25" x 31"
Block size: 3"

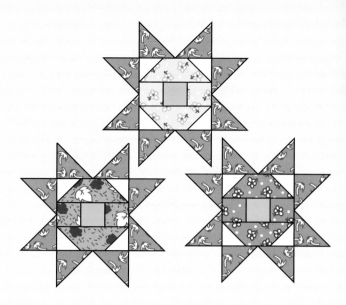

This sweet quilt, with flowers surrounded by interlocking stars, looks difficult to make, but take a moment to look over the directions and you'll see just how easy it is to construct. You can make this quilt in no time at all!

Fabric Requirements

⅝ yd. vintage white
⅜ yd. green print
6 fat quarters of assorted prints
Fat quarter yellow solid
⅔ yd. lavender print (border, binding)
⅞ yd. backing

Suggested Tool

Easy Scallop

Additional Supplies

Basic sewing supplies
Thread to match fabric
29" x 35" batting

Cutting Directions

FABRIC	CUT	TO YIELD
Vintage white	2—3½" x 40" strips	17—3½" squares
	3—2" x 40" strips	24—2" x 3½" rectangles
		4—2" squares
	3—1½" x 40" strips	72—1½" squares
From *each* fat quarter print	2—1½" x 20" strips	6—1½" x 3½" rectangles
		6—1½" squares
Yellow solid	2—1½" x 20" strips	18—1½" squares
Green print	5—2" x 40" strips	96—2" squares
Lavender print	3—4" x 40" strips	Borders
	1¼" bias strips	Binding

Sew exact ¼" seams throughout. Place fabrics right sides together for sewing, unless otherwise noted.

Assemble the Connector Blocks (Make 17)

1. In the same manner as in Step 3, sew the 2" green squares on the corners of the 3½" white squares. Press. At this point the blocks should measure 3½".

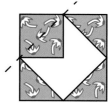

Make 17

2. In the same manner as Step 1, sew green squares to the corners of 14 white rectangles. Press.

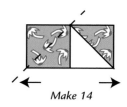

Make 14

Assemble the Flower Blocks (Make 18)

1. Sew a yellow square between two matching print squares. Press toward the print squares.

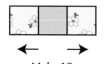

Make 18

2. Sew matching print rectangles to both sides of the units made in Step 1. Press toward the center. At this point the block should measure 3½" square.

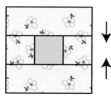

Make 18

3. Mark or crease a diagonal line on the wrong side of the white 1½" squares. Place the white 1½" squares on each corner of the blocks made in Step 2. Sew; trim the seam to ¼" and press toward the block center. At this point the block should still measure 3½".

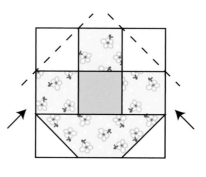

Make 18

Assemble the Quilt

Arrange the flower blocks alternated with the connector blocks in rows as shown below. Add the plain white rectangles, squares and pieced rectangles along the outer edges. Sew the units together in rows, pressing as shown.

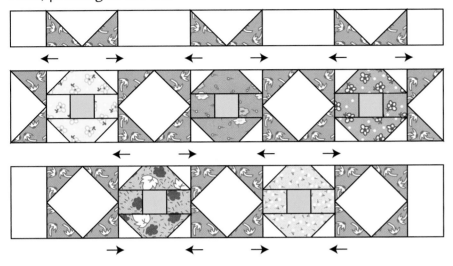

Borders

Refer to page 10 for detailed instructions on adding borders and page 126 for marking and binding a scalloped edge.

1. Measure and cut two borders the width of the quilt. Sew to the top and bottom of the quilt. Press toward the borders.

2. Repeat this procedure for the sides of the quilt. Press.

3. Mark a scalloped edge on the quilt top, rounding the corners. The scallops are marked at 5½" intervals.

Quilting Suggestions

To prepare the quilt for quilting, layer the backing (which has been cut at least 4" larger than the quilt top) wrong side up, followed by the batting (again, cut larger than the quilt top) and last, the quilt top, right-side up. Thread or pin baste in a 4" grid across the quilt. Quilt as desired.

The quilt shown was hand quilted in the ditch around each of the yellow flower centers. An "X" was hand quilted in the center of the connector blocks. A "V" was stitched in the plain white rectangles. A pretty flower design was quilted in the border.

Binding

1. Before binding, hand baste along the marked scalloped line.

2. Join the binding ends with diagonal seams pressed open.

3. Sew to the quilt, matching up the binding to the marked scallop line. Stitch a ¼" seam, pivoting at the "V" in each scallop.

4. Trim the excess batting and backing.

5. Turn the binding to the backside. Turn under ¼" and stitch down by hand with matching thread.

6. Sign and date.

Pansies in Bloom

Finished size: 25" square
Block size: 3"

Winters are long and dreary where I live in Minnesota, so we eagerly await spring and the return of green plants and blooming flowers. Pansies are one of my favorite flowers, as they bloom most of the (short) growing season in Minnesota, and always look spectacular! Stitching them into a quilt allows me to enjoy them indoors all year long.

If you can't find a pansy print for the border, any floral fabric will work. Just pull the colors from the focal print for your pansies. Pansies come in many colors! Use either solids or marbled prints or even batiks to give the flowers a more realistic look. I fused the flowers for a quick project, but you can appliqué them by hand.

Fabric Requirements	Suggested Tool	Additional Supplies
Fat quarter light floral background	Easy Scallop	Basic sewing supplies
Fat quarter light green print		Fusible web
½ yd. (or 2 fat quarters) light purple print		Embroidery floss in yellow and dark purple
4" x 12" piece dark purple print (pansies)		Thread to match fabric
4" x 12" piece yellow print (pansies)		29" x 29" batting
½ yd. pansy print (or other floral)		
⅞ yd. backing		

Cutting Directions

FABRIC	CUT	TO YIELD
Light floral background	3—3½" x 20" strips	12—3½" squares
	4—1½" x 20" strips	Strip sets
Light green print	5—1½" x 20" strips	Strip sets
Light purple print	4—1½" x 20" strips	Inside border
	1¼" bias strips	Binding
Pansy print	3—4½" x 40" strips	Outer border

Sew exact ¼" seams throughout. Place fabrics right sides together for sewing, unless otherwise noted.

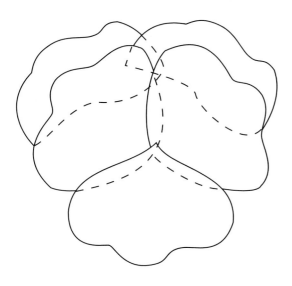

Assemble the Nine-Patch Blocks
(Make 13)

1. Sew together two strip sets of green, background, green. Press toward the green strips. Cut into 26 segments 1½".

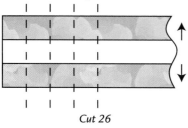

Cut 26

2. Sew together one strip set of background, green, background. Press toward the green strip. Cut into 13 segments 1½".

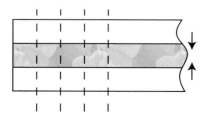

Cut 13

3. Sew the units from Step 1 and 2 together into 13 nine-patch blocks. Press. At this point the blocks should measure 3½".

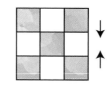

Make 13

Assemble the Pansy Block
(Make 12)

1. Trace the shapes the required number of times on the fusible web. Roughly cut out. Following the manufacturer's directions, fuse to the wrong side of the fabric chosen for the appliqué pieces. I chose to change the placement of the colors in each flower. You can make them all the same, if you prefer.

2. Starting at the back of the flower, overlap the petals and fuse into place on the 3½" background squares.

Assemble the Quilt

1. Sew the nine-patch blocks and the Pansy blocks together, alternating them in five rows as shown in the photo. Press toward the Pansy blocks.

2. Sew the rows together, pinning and matching seam intersections.

3. By hand or machine with matching thread or floss, stitch a small buttonhole stitch

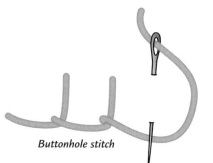

Buttonhole stitch

around the flower shapes. With two strands of embroidery floss, hand embroider the center on each flower. Use a satin stitch for the center and long straight stitches for the accents.

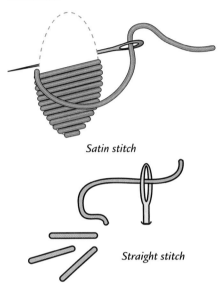

Satin stitch

Straight stitch

Borders

Refer to page 126 for detailed instructions on marking and binding a scalloped border.

1. Measure, cut and sew two narrow purple borders to the top and bottom of the quilt. Press toward the borders. Repeat for the side borders.

2. In the same manner, measure, cut and sew two wide pansy borders to the top and bottom of the quilt. Repeat for the sides of the quilt.

3. Mark the scalloped edge with rounded corners. The scallops are marked at 5" intervals.

Quilting Suggestions

To prepare the quilt for quilting, layer the backing (which has been cut at least 4" larger than the quilt top) wrong side up, followed by the batting (again, cut larger than the quilt top) and last, the quilt top, right-side up. Thread or pin baste in a 4" grid across the quilt. Quilt as desired. The quilt shown was hand quilted in the ditch around each of the pansies. Diagonal lines were quilted through the nine-patch blocks. A line of quilting also was stitched in the ditch between each of the borders. The pansies in the border fabric were outline quilted by machine.

Binding

1. Before binding, hand baste on the marked scallop line. Do NOT cut on that marked line!

2. Join the bias binding strips with diagonal seams pressed open.

3. Sew binding to the quilt with a ¼" seam.

4. After the binding is sewn on, trim excess batting and backing.

5. Turn the binding to the backside and stitch down by hand with matching thread.

6. Sign and date your sweet little quilt!

Pansy Pincushion

Finished size: 7" x 9½"

A lovely gift or just a pretty treat for you, this pansy pincushion is quick to make with scraps of wool and embroidery floss. Wool doesn't fray, so you don't have to turn under the edges. Just stitch and enjoy!

Fabric Requirements

⅓ yd. or 12" x 14" light lavender wool

Wool scraps: yellow, green, medium purple, dark purple

Note: You can use felted or unfelted wool.

Additional Supplies

Embroidery floss in yellow, green and lavender

Basic sewing supplies

Fiberfill

Freezer paper

Assembly Directions

1. Trace the large oval, with the scalloped edge, the inside oval and the pansy templates for the pincushion from pages 48 and 49 onto paper (you can use freezer paper). Cut out on the marked line. Pin the paper patterns to the right side of the wool pieces. Cut out carefully with a sharp scissors. (You do not have to add seam allowance.)

2. Lightly crease the lavender oval with the scalloped edges in half from both directions. Use the creases to help you center the flower petals and leaves. When satisfied with the arrangement, pin and baste through all the layers, holding the shapes in place.

3. Using two strands of floss, buttonhole stitch the petals in place. Start with lavender floss on the medium lavender petals (or the petals at the top of the flower). Continue with yellow floss on the yellow petals and lavender floss on the dark

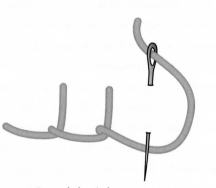

Buttonhole stitch

lavender petals. The leaves are buttonhole stitched with green floss around the edges and a running stitch through the center of the leaf.

4. Using lavender and yellow floss, satin stitch the center of the pansy, adding radiating lines in both colors.

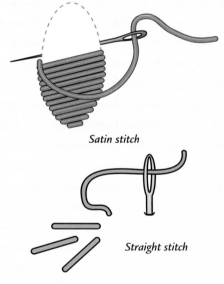

Satin stitch

Straight stitch

5. Using lavender floss, buttonhole stitch around the scalloped edges of the large oval.

Finish the Pincushion

1. Place the small lavender oval under the larger oval with wrong sides together. Center, pin and baste in place.

2. With two strands of lavender floss and the smaller oval on top, stitch the two pieces together with a running stitch, leaving an opening to stuff with wool or fiberfill. If desired, dried lavender could be added to the filling. When stuffed, finish stitching the two pieces together.

Pansy Pincushion

A Tisket, A Tasket

Finished size: 25" x 30"
Block size: 5" x 6½"

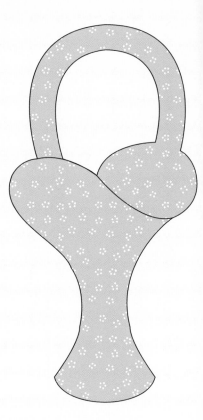

A tisket, a tasket, a pink polka basket.... Isn't that rhyme familiar? OK, maybe I changed it a bit. This sweet little quilt has a retro Art Deco designed basket; appliquéd in the peachy-pink color that also was very popular in that era. The basket is a smaller but similar version of the Peek-a-Boo Baskets from the "Granny Quilts" book.

This quilt is quick to make with only five appliqué blocks! If you can't find the same fabrics, choose any pretty floral for your border, and pull the colors from that print to make up the rest of the quilt.

Fabric Requirements
Fat quarter light yellow solid
Fat quarter yellow floral-stripe
½ yd. peach polka dots
½ yd. green-peach floral
⅞ yd. backing

Suggested Tool
Easy Scallop

Additional Supplies
Basic sewing supplies
Freezer paper or fusible web for appliqués
Liquid starch
Glue Baste-It
Thread to match fabric
Thread Heaven
29" x 34" batting

Cutting Directions

FABRIC	CUT	TO YIELD
Light yellow solid	3—5½" x 20" strips	5—5½" x 7" rectangles
Yellow floral-stripe	2—7" x 20" strips	4—5½" x 7" rectangles
Peach polka dot	2—1½" x 40" strips	Inner borders
	1¼" bias strips	Binding
Green-peach floral	1—2" x 40" strip	20—2" squares
	3—4½" x 40" strips	Outer border

Sew exact ¼" seams throughout. Place fabrics right sides together for sewing, unless otherwise noted.

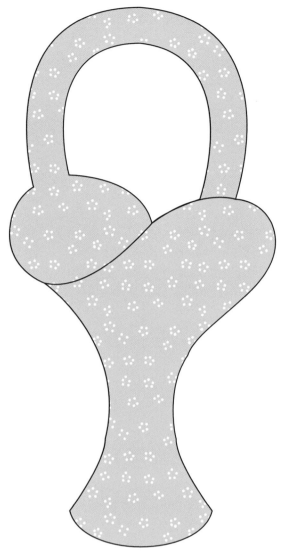

Assemble the Quilt

1. Join the appliquéd blocks to the yellow floral-stripe blocks as shown in the photo.

2. Press the seams toward the yellow floral-stripe blocks.

Borders

Refer to page 126 for detailed instructions for marking scalloped borders.

1. Measure the quilt through the middle, and cut two peach polka dot borders to this length. Sew to the top and bottom of the quilt, pressing toward the borders. Repeat for the other two sides of the quilt.

2. In the same manner, sew the wider green-peach floral borders to the quilt. Press toward the borders.

Appliqué Blocks
(Make 5)

Refer to page 13 for detailed instructions on freezer paper and fusible appliqué.

1. Trace the reversed design above onto the dull side of freezer paper or the paper side of fusible web. Cut out. Iron the basket templates to the wrong side of the peach polka dot fabric. Cut out, and fuse or appliqué the baskets to the yellow background rectangles.

2. With pencil, mark a diagonal line on the backside of each of the 2" green squares. With right sides together, place a green square on the corner of an appliquéd block. Stitch on the diagonal line. Trim the seam to ¼" and press toward the green corner. Repeat for all corners of the appliquéd blocks.

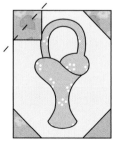

3. Using Easy Scallop, mark off one 7" scallop (with the largest size scallop tool) centered in the top and bottom borders. Mark a reversed 4" scallop (with the smaller scallop tool) on either side of the large scallop, ending with a 5" scallop at the corners. On the sides, centering the first scallop, mark a 7" (with the

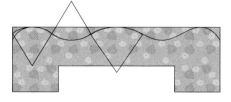

largest tool) scallop, then a reversed 7" scallop on both sides of it. Use a 5" scallop at the corners. Round each corner so they are identical.

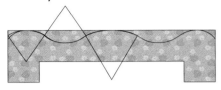

Quilting Suggestions

To prepare the quilt for quilting, layer the backing (which has been cut at least 4" larger than the quilt top) wrong side up, followed by the batting (again, cut larger than the quilt top) and last, the quilt top, right-side up. Thread or pin baste in a 4" grid across the quilt. Quilt as desired.

The quilt shown was hand quilted around the baskets and along the stripes in the yellow floral-stripe blocks. A line of hand quilting was stitched between the quilt and the borders and between the two borders. Crosshatching was quilted in the borders at 1" intervals.

Binding

Refer to page 126 for detailed instructions on binding scalloped edges.

1. Before stitching on the binding, hand baste on the marked scallop line. This prevents the layers from shifting while the binding is being sewn on.

2. To bind, join the bias strips with diagonal seams pressed open.

3. Sew the binding on with a ¼" seam. Trim the excess batting and backing.

4. Turn the binding to the backside and stitch down by hand with matching thread.

5. Sign and date your sweet little quilt!

Buttercup

Finished size: 26" x 32½"
Block size: 3"

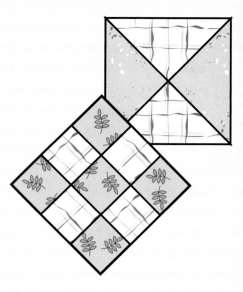

Blue and yellow, everyone's favorite color combination! This quilt was photographed in my friend Bonny's blue and yellow guest bedroom. It was the perfect accessory for this room. It is constructed of two simple blocks — a nine-patch and an hourglass block. Voila! A sweet little quilt, perfect for any room.

Fabric Requirements
⅓ yd. (or 1 fat quarter) yellow mottled
½ yd. blue print
⅓ yd. white-yellow plaid
⅔ yd. yellow-white floral-stripe (border)
⅞ yd. backing

Suggested Tools
Companion Angle
Easy Scallop

Note: If not using the Companion Angle, cut nine 4¼" squares. Cut twice on the diagonal. You will have two extra triangles from each fabric.

Additional Supplies
Basic sewing supplies
Thread to match fabric
30" x 37" batting

Cutting Directions

FABRIC	CUT	TO YIELD
Yellow mottled	2—2" x 40" strips	34 Companion Angle triangles*
	2—1½" x 40" strips	Inner borders
White-yellow plaid	2—2" x 40" strips	34 Companion Angle triangles*
	4—1½" x 40" strips	Strip sets
Blue print	5—1½" x 40" strips	Strip sets
		4—1½" squares (border corners)
	1¼" bias strips	Binding
Yellow-white floral-stripe	4—5" strips	Border

Layer the 2" white-yellow plaid and the 2" yellow mottled strips with right sides together. Cut with the Companion Angle. They are now ready to chain-sew.

Sew exact ¼" seams throughout. Place fabrics right sides together for sewing, unless otherwise noted.

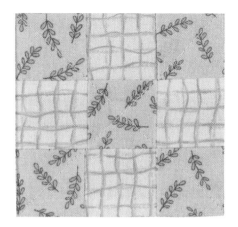

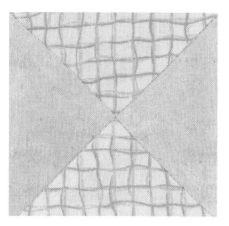

Assemble the Nine-Patch blocks (Make 18)

1. Sew together two strip sets of blue, plaid, blue. Press toward the blue fabrics.

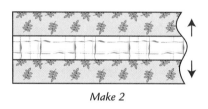

Make 2

2. Cut into 36 segments 1½" wide.

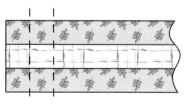

Cut 36

3. Sew together one strip set of plaid, blue, plaid. Press toward the blue strip. Cut into 18 segments 1½" wide.

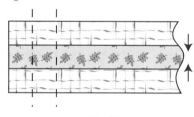

Cut 18

4. Matching and pinning the seam intersections, sew two Step 2 segments on either side of a Step 3 segment. Press. At this point the blocks should measure 3½".

Make 18 blocks

Assemble the Hourglass blocks (Make 17)

1. With the yellow-white plaid fabric on top, sew on the right-hand side of the triangles as shown (A). Keep the yellow-white plaid fabric on top each time (B). Press.

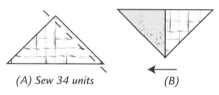

(A) Sew 34 units   *(B)*

2. Matching and pinning the center and points, sew two units from Step 1 together. Trim the "dog-ears." Twist the seam where it intersects to open it. Press. Refer to page 10 for more instruction on this technique. At this point the blocks should measure 3½".

Make 17 blocks

Assemble the Quilt

1. Sew four rows with three nine-patch blocks and two hourglass blocks. Watch the orientation of the hourglass blocks! Press toward the hourglass blocks.

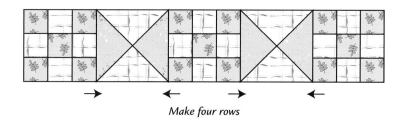

Make four rows

2. Sew three rows of two nine-patch blocks and three hourglass blocks. Watch the orientation of the hourglass blocks! Press toward the hourglass blocks.

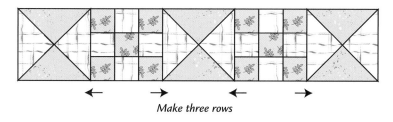

Make three rows

3. Alternate the rows from Step 1 and Step 2, referring to the quilt photo on page 59. Sew the rows together, matching and pinning at the seam intersections. Press the seams toward the Step 2 rows.

Borders

Refer to page 10 for detailed instructions on adding borders.
1. Measure and cut two 1½" yellow mottled borders the width of the quilt, and two 1½" yellow mottled borders the length of the quilt. Sew the first set of borders to the top and bottom of the quilt. Press toward the borders.

2. Sew the 1½" blue squares to both ends of the side borders. Press toward the borders. Sew to the sides of the quilt. Press toward the borders.

3. Measure and cut two yellow-white floral borders the width of the quilt plus 14". Set aside. Repeat for the length of the quilt, adding the extra 14". Mark the center of the borders and the exact width and length of the quilt. Match and pin the borders to the quilt. Sew, leaving ¼" from each corner unstitched. Miter the corners.

Mark the Scalloped Edge

Refer to page 126 for detailed instructions on marking a scalloped edge.
Before quilting, mark the scalloped edge on the quilt top. The quilt shown was marked in 5¼" scallops, with the corners left square.

Quilting Suggestions

To prepare the quilt for quilting, layer the backing (which has been cut at least 4" larger than the quilt top) wrong side up, followed by the batting (again, cut larger than the quilt top) and last, the quilt top, right-side up. Thread or pin baste in a 4" grid across the quilt. Quilt as desired.

The quilt shown was machine quilted in the diagonals of the hourglass blocks and on the diagonals in the nine-patch blocks. I also stitched on both sides of the inner border and in the stripes in the outer border.

Binding

Refer to page 126 for detailed instructions on binding a scalloped edge.
1. Before binding, hand baste along the marked scalloped line. Do NOT cut on this line! The basting will prevent the layers from shifting while the binding is being sewn on.

2. Join the single-bias binding strips with diagonal seams pressed open.

3. Align the binding edge to the marked scalloped edge, stitching a ¼" seam. Stitch until you reach the bottom of the "V," stop, lift the presser foot, and pivot with the needle down, pushing any pleats that form behind the needle. Put the presser foot back down and stitch out of the "V." (Gently ease the binding around the curves; do not stretch.) Miter the square corners.

4. Trim the excess batting and backing.

5. Turn the binding to the backside and turn the binding under ¼". Stitch down by hand with matching thread.

6. Sign and date your little beauty!

Dances with Bears

Finished size: 22½" x 25½"
Block size: 3"

A "twist" on an old favorite, this quilt takes the basic Bear's Paw block for a spin!

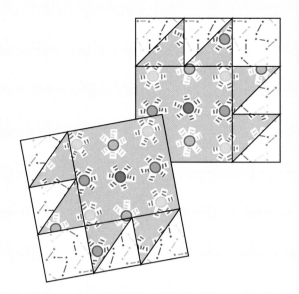

Fabric Requirements

Fat quarter background print
3" x 16" pieces of 15 assorted prints
Fat quarter (or ¼ yd. to avoid piecing) (border)
Fat quarter (binding)
¾ yd. backing

Suggested Tools

Easy Angle
Easy Scallop
Note: If not using the Easy Angle, cut 1⅞" squares. Cut once on the diagonal.

Additional Supplies

Basic sewing supplies
Thread to match fabric
27" x 30" batting

Cutting Directions

FABRIC	CUT	TO YIELD
Background	10—1½" x 20" strips	30—1½" squares
		120 Easy Angle triangles*
From *each* of the assorted prints	1—2½" x 16" strip	2—2½" squares
		Trim remainder of strip to 1½", cut: eight Easy Angle triangles*
Border print	2—4" x 40" strips	Borders
Binding	1¼" bias strips	Binding

Layer background and print strips with right sides together. Cut with the Easy Angle. They are now ready to chain-sew.

Sew exact ¼" seams throughout. Place fabrics right sides together for sewing, unless otherwise noted.

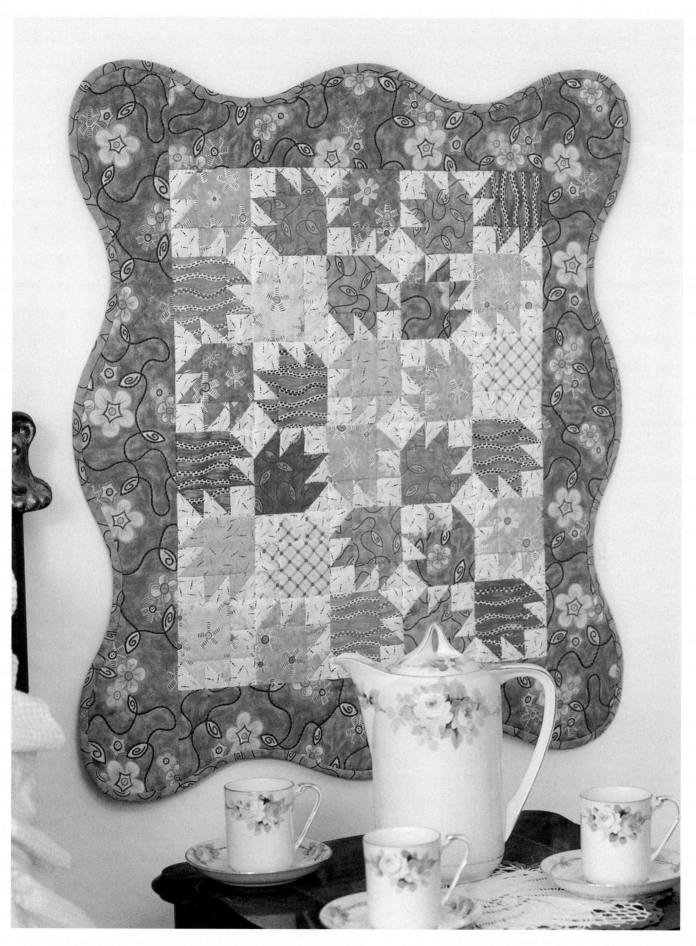

Assemble the Blocks
(Make 30)

1. Chain-sew all the triangle squares. Press toward the print triangle. Trim "dog-ears."

2. Sew two matching triangles together; press.

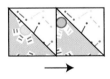

3. Sew a Step 2 unit to the side of a matching square. Press.

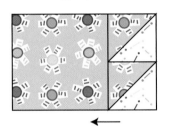

4. Sew two matching triangles together, then add a background square to one end. Press.

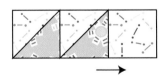

5. Sew the Step 4 unit to the top of the Step 3 unit. Press. At this point the blocks should measure 3½".

6. Repeat Steps 1 through 5 to make a total of 30 blocks.

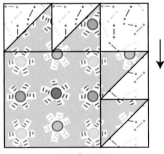

Make 30

 TIP: Twist the seam where it intersects to open it. Press. Refer to page 10 for more instruction on this technique.

Assemble the Quilt

1. Using the photo on page 61 as a guide, arrange the blocks in rows. There are only two different rows. Make three rows of each as shown below.

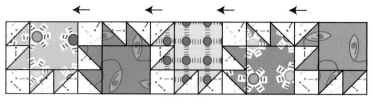

Make three

2. Make three rows as shown.

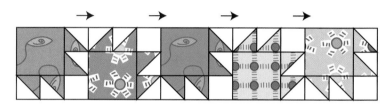

Make three

3. Press the seams towards the large squares. Sew the rows together, matching and pinning at seam intersections.

Borders

Refer to page 10 for detailed instructions on adding borders.
Measure, then trim two borders the width of the quilt. Sew to the top and bottom of the quilt. Repeat for the sides of the quilt.

Mark the Wavy Edge

Refer to page 126 for detailed instructions on marking scallops.
Mark a wavy edge on the quilt. For the quilt shown, the top and bottom were marked with a 4½" scallop, starting with a full scallop at one edge and reversing the scallop tool on alternate scallops. The side borders were marked with 5" scallops.

Quilting Suggestions

To prepare the quilt for quilting, layer the backing (which has been cut at least 4" larger than the quilt top) wrong side up, followed by the batting (again, cut larger than the quilt top) and last, the quilt top, right-side up. Thread or pin baste in a 4" grid across the quilt. Quilt as desired. The quilt shown was stitched in the ditch around each of the blocks and around the squares in each Bear's Paw. The border was quilted following the vine in the border print.

Binding

Refer to page 126 for detailed instructions on binding a scalloped or curved edge.
1. Before binding, baste on the marked wavy edge. Do NOT cut on this edge.

2. Join the binding strips with diagonal seams pressed open.

3. Sew the binding strips to the quilt with a ¼" seam, easing around the inside and outside curves.

4. Trim off excess batting and backing.

5. Turn the binding to the back of the quilt. Turn the binding under ¼" and stitch down by hand with matching thread.

6. Sign and date your quilt.

Posy Patch

Finished size: 22" square
Block size: 7½"

Choose some pretty floral fabrics (perhaps one of those fat quarter bundles you bought!) to make up this little quilt. There are only four blocks, so it sews together quickly.

Fabric Requirements
Fat quarter large floral
Fat quarter light floral background
Fat quarter green tonal
Fat quarter rose tonal
¾ yd. backing

Suggested Tool
Easy Angle
Note: If not using the Easy Angle, cut 16 squares 1⅞". Cut once on the diagonal.

Additional Supplies
Basic sewing supplies
Thread to match fabric
26" x 26" batting

Cutting Directions

FABRIC	CUT	TO YIELD
Large floral	Fussy cut 4—5½" squares	
Light floral background	2—1½" x 20" strips	32 Easy Angle triangles*
	4—1½" x 20" strips	16—1½" x 3½" rectangles
	6—1½" x 20" strips	12—1½" x 7½" rectangles
Green tonal	2—2½" x 20" strips	16—2½" squares
	2—1½" x 20" strips	32 Easy Angle triangles*
	5—1¼" x 20" strips	Binding
Rose tonal	2—1½" x 20" strips	25—1½" squares
	4—2½" x 20" strips	Outer border

Note: Layer the background and green 1½" strips with right sides together. Cut with the Easy Angle. They are now ready to chain-sew.

Sew exact ¼" seams throughout. Place fabrics right sides together for sewing, unless otherwise noted.

Block Assembly
(Make 4)

1. Mark a diagonal line on the wrong side of the 2½" green squares. Place a square on a corner of the large fussy-cut floral square and sew on the diagonal line. Repeat at each corner of each large square. Trim the seam allowance to ¼". Press toward the green triangle.

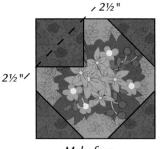

Make four

2. Sew the triangle-squares together. Press toward the green triangle.

Make 32

3. Sew a light background 1½" x 3½" rectangle between two triangle-squares. Press toward the light rectangle.

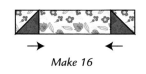

Make 16

4. Sew the units from Step 3 to the top and bottom of the units from Step 1. Press toward the Step 3 units.

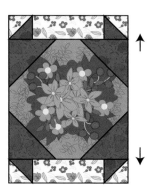

Make four

5. Sew the rose tonal squares to both ends of the remaining Step 3 units. Press toward the Step 3 units.

Make eight

6. Sew the Step 5 units to the Step 4 units. Press toward the center of the block. At this point the block should measure 7½".

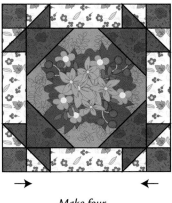

Make four

Assemble the Quilt

1. Sew three light floral background 1½" x 7½" sashing rectangles between two blocks and on both ends. Press toward the sashing.

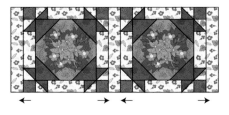

Make two

2. Sew three rose tonal squares and two light floral background rectangles together for horizontal sashing rows. Press toward the sashing rectangles.

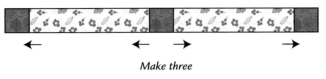

Make three

3. Sew the horizontal sashing rows between the block rows and to the top and bottom of the quilt. See photo below for placement. Press the seams toward the sashing.

Borders

Refer to page 10 for detailed instructions on adding borders.

1. Measure, cut and sew rose tonal borders to the top and bottom of the quilt. Press toward the borders.

2. In the same manner, cut and sew rose tonal borders to the sides of the quilt. Press toward the borders.

3. Measure and place a dot 2½" from each corner along the outside edge. Draw a line connecting those dots at a corner. Trim on the marked 2½" lines.

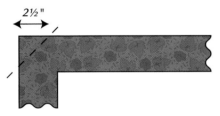

2½"

Quilting Suggestions

To prepare the quilt for quilting, layer the backing (which has been cut at least 4" larger than the quilt top) wrong side up, followed by the batting (again, cut larger than the quilt top) and last, the quilt top, right-side up. Thread or pin baste in a 4" grid across the quilt. Quilt as desired. The quilt shown was hand quilted, outlining some of the motifs in the floral bouquet. It was machine stitched in the ditch around the large square. The floral background was machine meandered and a simple cable design was hand quilted in the border.

Binding

Refer to page 11 for detailed instructions on binding a quilt.

1. Before binding, hand baste a scant ¼" from the edge of the quilt. This prevents the layers from shifting while the binding is being sewn on.

2. Join the binding strips with ¼" diagonal seams pressed open.

3. Sew the binding to the quilt with a ¼" seam. Trim excess batting and backing.

4. Turn the binding over to the backside and turn under ¼". Stitch down by hand.

Sunshine and Lavender

Finished size: 17¾ x 20½"
Block size: 2"

   This darling little quilt is as refreshing as a whiff of lavender and as cheerful as a ray of sunshine on a cloudy day. Purchase some lavender and yellow fat quarters on your next visit to a quilt shop. Make up this quick little quilt to bring a smile to your face, or give it to someone you love. It will surely brighten their day!

Fabric Requirements

Fat quarter light floral background
Fat quarter yellow floral
Fat quarter light lavender floral
Fat quarter dark lavender tonal
⅝ yd. backing

Suggested Tools

Easy Angle
Companion Angle
Note: If not using the Easy Angle, cut 1⅞" squares. Cut once on the diagonal. If not using the Companion Angle, cut 4¼" squares. Cut twice on the diagonal.

Additional Supplies

Basic sewing supplies
Thread to match fabric
22" x 25" batting

Cutting Directions

FABRIC	CUT	TO YIELD
Light floral background	5—1½" x 20" strips	80 Easy Angle triangles*
	1—2½" x 20" strip	2—2½" squares, cut once on the diagonal (corners)
	2—2" x 20" strips	14 Companion Angle triangles (setting triangles)
Yellow floral	2—2½" x 20" strips	12—2½" squares
	4—1½" x 20" strips	Middle border
Light lavender floral	3—1½" x 20" strips	40 Easy Angle triangles*
	4—2½" x 20" strips	Outer border
Dark lavender tonal	3—1½" x 20" strips	40 Easy Angle triangles*
	4—1½" x 20" strips	Inner border
	4—1¼" x 20" strips	Binding

Note: Layer the 1½" light and dark lavender strips, with right sides together, with the light floral background strips. Cut with the Easy Angle. The triangle squares will then be ready to chain-sew.

Sew exact ¼" seams throughout. Place fabrics right sides together for sewing, unless otherwise noted.

Pinwheel Block Assembly (Make 20)

1. Sew the triangle squares together (A). Press toward the darker fabric. Join a light lavender triangle square together with a dark lavender triangle square to make a pair (B). Press toward the lighter triangle square.

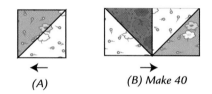

(A)   (B) Make 40

2. Join the pairs to make pinwheel blocks. Twist the seam where it intersects to open it. Press. Refer to page 10 for more instruction on this technique. At this point the blocks should measure 2½".

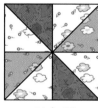

Make 20

3. Referring to the photo on page 71, orient the pinwheel blocks on the diagonal as shown. Alternate with yellow squares. Finish the ends of the rows with light floral triangles. Sew the blocks and triangles in rows. Press toward the yellow squares and setting triangles.

4. Sew the rows together. Press the seams all one direction.

5. Add the smaller corner triangles last. Note the setting and corner triangles are larger than needed.

6. Trim the edges of the quilt, making certain to leave at least ¼" seam allowance around the edge.

Borders

Refer to page 10 for detailed instructions on adding borders.

1. Measure, cut and sew two dark lavender inner borders to the top and bottom of the quilt. Press toward the borders. Repeat this procedure for the sides of the quilt.

2. Repeat Step 1 for adding the narrow yellow middle borders to the quilt. Press toward the yellow borders. Repeat this procedure for the light lavender outer borders. Press toward the lavender borders.

Quilting Suggestions

To prepare the quilt for quilting, layer the backing (which has been cut at least 4" larger than the quilt top) wrong side up, followed by the batting (again, cut larger than the quilt top) and last, the quilt top, right-side up. Thread or pin baste in a 4" grid across the quilt. Quilt as desired. The quilt shown was machine quilted in diagonal lines through the pinwheel and the yellow blocks, and into the light floral setting triangles. A line of stitching was quilted in the ditch between each of the borders. A design was hand quilted in the outer border.

Binding

Refer to page 11 for detailed instructions on binding a quilt.

1. Before binding, hand baste a scant ¼" from the edge of the quilt. This prevents the layers from shifting while the binding is being sewn on.

2. Bind with the dark lavender 1¼" strips, joined with diagonal seams pressed open.

3. Sew to the quilt with a ¼" seam. Trim excess batting and backing.

4. Turn the binding to the backside of the quilt. Turn under ¼" and stitch down by hand with matching thread.

5. Sign and date your little quilt!

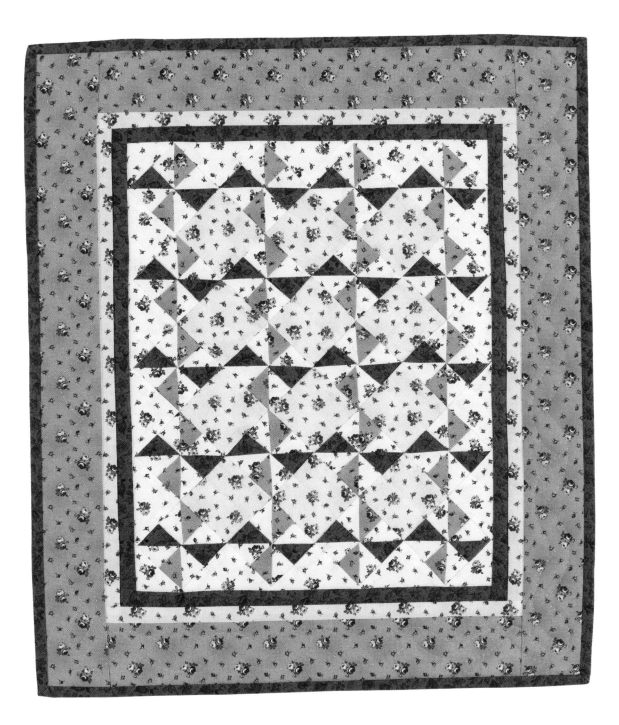

Sweet Lavender

Finished size: 23" x 27½"
Block size: 4¼"

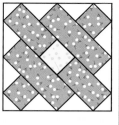
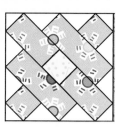

English Lavender is one of my favorite plants in my flower garden. It's not a showy plant, but the scent is lovely and calming to the spirit. The color lavender is also soft, sweet and feminine. Using the lavender flower and the color lavender as my inspiration, I created this Sweet Lavender quilt.

The block is a simplified version of a block called Album or Chimney Sweep. The original block has a larger center area for signing names. I wanted the block to look more like a flower, so I reduced the center to one square. The alternate version of this quilt in indigos (see page 78) is a more typical coloration for the Album or Chimney Sweep block.

Fabric Requirements

Fat quarter light print
6 fat quarters of assorted prints
2" x 21" yellow print (block centers)
Fat quarter green print (sashing)
Fat quarter green print (binding)
½ yd. lavender print
¾ yd. backing

Suggested Tools

Companion Angle
Easy Angle
Easy Scallop
Note: If not using the Companion Angle, cut 24 squares 2¾". Cut twice on the diagonal. If not using the Easy Angle, cut 24 squares 1⅞". Cut once on the diagonal.

Additional Supplies

Basic sewing supplies
Thread to match fabric
27" x 32" batting

Cutting Directions

FABRIC	CUT	TO YIELD
Light print	8—1¼" x 20" strips	96 Companion Angle triangles
	3—1½" x 20" strips	48 Easy Angle triangles
From *each* of six fat quarter prints	2—1½" x 20" strips	4—1½" x 3½" rectangles
		4—1½" x 2½" rectangles
		4—1½" squares
Yellow print*	1½" x 20" strip	12—1½" squares
Green print 1	5—1" x 20" strips	17—1" x 4¾" sashes
	4—1" x 20" strips	Inside borders
Lavender print	1" x 7" strip	6—1" squares (cornerstones)
	3—4½" x 40" strips	Outside borders
Green print 2	1¼" bias strips	Binding

*Note: I chose to use a pink print for the centers of the yellow blocks.

Sew exact ¼" seams throughout. Place fabrics right sides together for sewing, unless otherwise noted.

Flower Block Assembly
(Make 12)

1. Sew light Companion Angle triangles to both sides of the 1½" print squares (A) and the 1½" x 3½" print rectangles as shown (B). Press toward the squares or rectangles. Note the triangles are larger than needed.

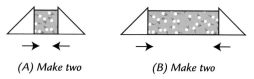

(A) Make two   (B) Make two

2. Sew a yellow square between the two 1½" x 2½" print rectangles. Press toward the yellow square.

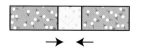

3. Sew the Step 1 units together in pairs (A). Add a Step 2 unit to one of the pairs (B). Press.

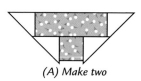

(A) Make two

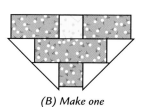

(B) Make one

4. Sew the two units from Step 3 together. Press toward the center. Add smaller light Easy Angle triangles to all four corners. Note the corner triangles are larger than needed. Press toward the center. **Trim the blocks evenly to measure 4¾" square.**

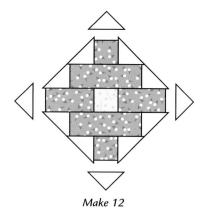

Make 12

5. Repeat to make a total of 12 blocks.

Assemble the Quilt Top

1. Sew two green sashing strips between three blocks. Press toward the sashing.

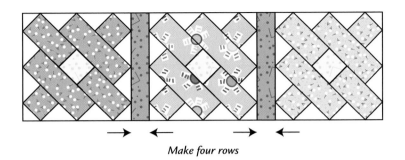

Make four rows

2. Sew three green sashing strips to two lavender cornerstones. Press toward the sashing.

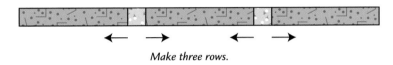

Make three rows.

3. Sew the block rows and sashing rows together. Press toward the sashing rows.

Borders

Refer to page 126 for detailed instructions on marking scalloped borders.

1. Measure, cut and sew two narrow green borders to the top of the quilt. Press toward the borders. Repeat for the sides of the quilt.

2. In the same manner, sew 4½" lavender borders to the top, bottom and sides of the quilt, pressing toward the borders.

3. Mark a scalloped border on the quilt. The quilt shown was marked with 5½" scallops.

Quilting Suggestions

1. To prepare the quilt for quilting, layer the backing (which has been cut at least 4" larger than the quilt top) wrong side up, followed by the batting (again, cut larger than the quilt top) and last, the quilt top, right-side up. Thread or pin baste in a 4" grid across the quilt. Quilt as desired.

The quilt shown was machine stitched in the ditch around each of the blocks and between the two borders. A line of hand quilting was stitched ¼" from the seams in the "flowers." A flowing feather design was hand quilted in the border.

Binding

Refer to page 126 for detailed instructions on binding a scalloped edge.

1. Before binding, baste on the marked scallop line to hold the three layers together.

2. Sew the bias binding strips together with diagonal seams pressed open. Sew to the quilt with a ¼" seam.

3. Trim the excess batting and backing.

4. Turn the binding to the backside. Turn the binding under ¼" and stitch down by hand with matching thread.

5. Sign and date your lovely Sweet Lavender quilt!

Lavender Blue

Finished size: 21" x 25½"
Block size: 4¼"

This is the same pattern as Sweet Lavender on page 72, but it looks totally different in this coloration. Indigos (dark blue prints) and shirtings (white with small do-dads of color) were popular fabrics around the turn of the century. Today, blue and white quilts are considered classic quilts.

Isn't it fun to try other color ways for the same pattern? These little quilts make up so quickly; you can really let your imagination (or your stash) dictate your fabric choices.

Fabric Requirements
Fat quarter light print
6 fat quarters of assorted indigo prints
Fat quarter red print (sashing)
⅝ yd. indigo print (border, binding)
¾ yd. backing

Suggested Tools
Companion Angle
Easy Angle
Note: If not using the Companion Angle, cut 24 squares 2¾". Cut twice on the diagonal.
If not using the Easy Angle, cut 24 squares 1⅞". Cut once on the diagonal.

Additional Supplies
Basic sewing supplies
Thread to match fabric
25" x 30" batting

Cutting Directions

FABRIC	CUT	TO YIELD
Light print	8—1¼" x 20" strips	96 Companion Angle triangles
	4—1½" x 20" strips	48 Easy Angle triangles
		12—1½" squares
From *each* of six indigo fat quarter prints (enough for two blocks)	2—1½" x 20" strips	4—1½" x 3½" rectangles
		4—1½" x 2½" rectangles
		4—1½" squares
From one indigo print	6—1" squares	Cornerstones
Red print	5—1" x 20" strips	17—1" x 4¾" sashes
	4—1" x 20" strips	Inside borders
Indigo print	3—3½" x 40" strips	Outside borders
	3—2" x 40" strips	Binding

Sew exact ¼" seams throughout. Place fabrics right sides together for sewing, unless otherwise noted.

Quilt Directions

1. Refer to the Sweet Lavender instructions on pages 72 through 77, but omit the scalloped edge treatment. Bind in straight-of-grain double binding.

2. The quilt shown was quilted in the same manner as Sweet Lavender, except a cable design was quilted in the border.

3. Don't forget to sign and date!

Cinnamon Pink

Finished size: 14½" x 18½"
Block size: 2"

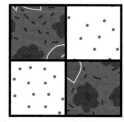

In the 1800s, a popular color scheme for quilts was pink and brown. At that time there were many brown prints available. Now, a hundred or more years later, we find the mordant used in the dyeing process is rotting the fabrics. Double-pinks, or pink prints on a pink ground, have been available since at least the early 1800s, and are considered very colorfast. These pink prints were so popular in some communities they were labeled "slave pink" or "Methodist pink," or whatever racial, ethnic or religious group in the area was the butt of the jokes.

Shirting prints (white prints with a tiny figure) instead of muslin were often used in quilts during this time. Women made blouses (or "waists" as they were called back then), men's shirts and children's clothing from these shirting fabrics. They would use the scraps from the clothing in their quilt making.

Four-patches are the most basic unit of patchwork, and often were a young girl's first sewing project. Sometimes they would piece a small quilt for their dolls or baby brother or sister.

This quilt is made in the style of those older quilts, inspired by a vintage full-size quilt in my collection that had the same size blocks!

With only three fabrics and simple patchwork, this could be a first project for you, a daughter or a granddaughter.

Fabric Requirements

Fat quarter double-pink print
Fat quarter brown print
Fat quarter shirting print
½ yd. backing

Additional Supplies

Basic sewing supplies
Thread to match fabric
18" x 23" batting

Cutting Directions

FABRIC	CUT	TO YIELD
Shirting print	4—1½" x 20" strips	Strip sets
Brown print	4—1½" x 20" strips	Strip sets
	3—2½" x 20" strips	Borders
Double-pink print	3—2½" x 20" strips	17—2½" squares
	4—2" x 20" strips	Binding

Sew exact ¼" seams throughout. Place fabrics right sides together for sewing, unless otherwise noted.

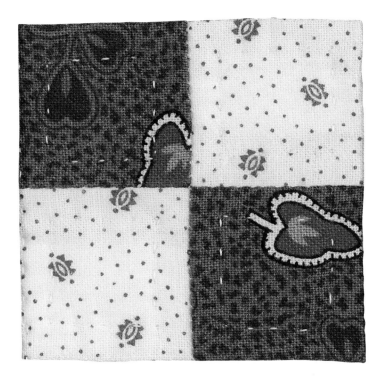

Four-Patch Assembly (Make 22 blocks)

1. Sew together the long edges of the shirting and brown print 1½" strips. Press toward the brown strip. Make four strip sets.

2. Cut into 44 units 1½".

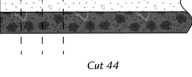

Cut 44

3. Sew the units into 22 four-patches. Twist the seam where it intersects to open it. Press. Refer to page 10 for more instruction on this technique.

4. At this point the blocks should measure 2½".

Sew 22

 TIP: Finger-press the seam to the dark fabric, and then iron, being careful to keep the strip set straight.

5. Sew together a row of three four-patches and two pink squares, pressing toward the pink squares.

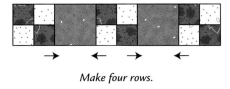

Make four rows.

6. Sew together a row of two four-patches and three pink squares, pressing toward the pink squares.

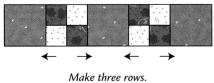

Make three rows.

7. Alternating the rows, sew the quilt top together. Press the seams all one direction.

Borders

Refer to page 10 for detailed instructions on adding borders.

1. Measure and cut two borders the width of the quilt and two borders the length of the quilt. Sew top and bottom borders to the quilt; press toward the borders.

2. Sew the remaining four-patches to both ends of the side borders, orienting them as shown in the photo. Press toward the borders.

3. Sew the side borders to the quilt. Press the seams toward the borders.

Quilting Suggestions

Mark any quilting designs. To prepare the quilt for quilting, layer the backing (which has been cut at least 4" larger than the quilt top) wrong side up, followed by the batting (again, cut larger than the quilt top) and last, the quilt top, right-side up. Thread or pin baste in a 4" grid across the quilt. The quilt shown was hand quilted inside each of the squares in the four-patches and an "X" was quilted in the pink squares. A cable design was quilted in the border.

Binding

Refer to page 11 for detailed instructions on binding a quilt.

1. Before binding, hand baste a scant ¼" from the edge of the quilt to keep the layers from shifting as the binding is sewn on.

2. Join the double-binding strips with diagonal seams pressed open.

3. Fold the binding in half lengthwise with wrong sides together. Press.

4. Sew the binding to the quilt with a ¼" seam. Trim excess batting and backing.

5. Turn the binding to the backside and stitch down by hand with matching thread.

6. Sign and date your "vintage" quilt.

Spinning Stars

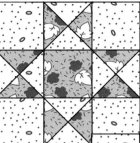
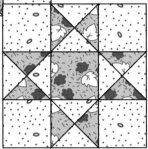

Finished size: 17½" x 22"
Block size: 3"

Using reproduction fabrics from the 1800s (Civil War era and later) I made two versions of this Spinning Star quilt. The blocks are quite easy to make. The alternate plain block setting is quick to piece together (no block seams to match!). Try making this quilt in your favorite fabrics, or use one of those many fat quarter bundles you've collected!

Fabric Requirements

Fat quarter light background
Fat quarter medium print
   (alternate blocks, setting
   triangles)
6 fat quarters of coordinating
   prints
Fat quarter coordinating print
   (border, binding)
⅝ yd. backing

Suggested Tool

Companion Angle
Note: If not using the Companion Angle, cut 2¼" and 6¼" squares, respectively. Cut twice on the diagonal to make triangles.

Additional Supplies

Basic sewing supplies
Thread to match fabric
22" x 26" batting

Cutting Directions

FABRIC	CUT	TO YIELD
Light background	4—1½" x 20" strips	48—1½" squares
	6—1" x 20" strips	96 Companion Angle triangles*
From *each* of the six fat quarter coordinating prints	1—1½" x 20" strip	10—1½" squares
	1—1" x 20" strip	16 Companion Angle triangles*
Medium print	2—3½" x 20" strips	8—3½" squares
	2—3" x 20" strips	10 Companion Angle triangles
Border print	4—2½" x 20" strips	Borders
	4—1¼" x 20" strips	Single, straight-of-grain binding

Note: Layer 1" background and print strips with right sides together. Cut the Companion Angle triangles. They are now ready to chain-sew.

Sew exact ¼" seams throughout. Place fabrics right sides together for sewing, unless otherwise noted.

Spinning Stars I

Block Assembly
(Make 12)

1. With the print on top and sewing on the right side, chain-sew all the small Companion Angle triangles together (A). Press toward the print triangle (B).

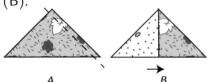

A   B

TIP: Sew together only one hourglass unit before chain-sewing all of them. When the hourglass unit is complete, it should be the same size as the 1½" squares. If not, you need to adjust your seam allowance accordingly.

2. Sew the Step 1 units together to make hourglass units. Twist the seam where it intersects to open it. Press. Refer to page 10 for more instruction on this technique. Make 48 hourglass units.

Make 48

3. Join four matching pieced hourglass units, four 1½" background squares and one matching print square, to make a star block. Press the units as indicated. At this point the blocks should measure 3½".

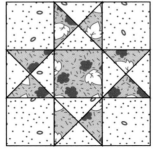

Make 12 blocks

4. Mark diagonal lines on the wrong side of each of the remaining print squares. Place a matching print square on the corner of a block. Sew on the diagonal. Trim the seam to ¼", press toward the dark triangle. Repeat on each corner of each block. At this point the blocks should measure 3½".

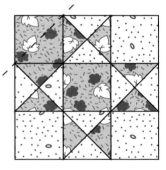

Make 12 blocks

Spinning Stars II

Quilt Assembly

1. Arrange the pieced blocks and medium print squares in diagonal rows. Use the photo on the previous page for guidance. Add the medium print triangles along the side edges. Cut the remaining two medium print squares in half once on the diagonal to make the corner triangles. (Note the setting and corner triangles are larger than needed.)

2. Sew the blocks, alternate squares and setting triangles together in diagonal rows. Press toward the alternate squares and triangles.

3. Sew the diagonal rows together. Press the seams all one direction. Add the corner triangles last. Press.

4. Trim the edges of the quilt evenly, making certain to leave at least a ¼" seam allowance from the corners of the blocks. Keep the corners square.

Borders

Refer to page 10 for detailed instructions on adding borders.

1. Measure and cut two borders the *length* of the quilt. (It's important to add the sides first or the border strips won't be long enough.)

2. Sew to the sides of the quilt. Press toward the borders. Repeat for the top and bottom of the quilt.

Quilting Suggestions

To prepare the quilt for quilting, layer the backing (which has been cut at least 4" larger than the quilt top) wrong side up, followed by the batting (again, cut larger than the quilt top) and last, the quilt top, right-side up. Thread or pin baste in a 4" grid across the quilt. Quilt as desired. The quilts shown were hand quilted in a 1" grid following the seam lines in the blocks and through the alternate blocks as well. A simple design was hand quilted in the border.

Binding

Refer to page 11 for detailed instructions on binding a quilt.

1. Before binding, hand baste a scant ¼" around the edge of the quilt to prevent the layers from shifting when the binding is sewn on.

2. Join the binding strips with diagonal seams pressed open. Sew to the quilt with a ¼" seam.

3. Trim the batting and backing.

4. Turn the binding to the backside of the quilt. Turn the binding under ¼" and stitch down by hand with matching thread.

5. Sign and date your quilt.

Vintage Doll Quilt

Finished size: 18" x 22"

Vintage baby or doll quilts are hard to find and can be quite expensive to buy. Have you ever coveted one, but couldn't afford the price? A vintage doll or baby quilt from the turn of the century in good condition can sell for $100 to $1,000! Why? A hundred years ago women often had large families and no conveniences. If they did find the time to make a baby or doll quilt, most likely it would have seen hard use with numerous children.

Sometimes a girl's first piecing project would have been a four-patch or nine-patch block, two of the most basic quilt blocks. These little blocks may have ended up in a doll quilt.

My little quilt is NOT a vintage doll quilt, but made to look like one. I had an extra pieced strip from a larger vintage strippy quilt, and I "recycled" it into this little doll quilt. Basically, it is made up of nine-patches sewn together into long strips. The nine-patches were hand sewn, and are not terribly accurate. I did not try to "fix" the strips, but rather left them as they were, added the sashes and narrow border, and finished it.

If you want your little quilt to have an authentic vintage look, try piecing and quilting with less accuracy than usual. Take a casual approach! I also used a lightweight, soft batting (flannel can be used) and washed the quilt a number of times after completing to give it the patina of age.

Fabric Requirements

⅜ yd. indigo print (sashes, border, binding)
6 fat quarters of assorted prints*
⅝ yd. backing
*Note: For an authentic look, use reproduction indigos, gray (mourning) prints, woven plaids, stripes, a few old browns, double-pinks and burgundy-red prints.

Additional Supplies

Basic sewing supplies
Thread to match fabric
22" x 26" batting

TIP: Occasionally you can find a set of vintage four-patch or nine-patch blocks; these could be used with this pattern to make up a "vintage" doll or baby quilt.

Cutting Directions

FABRIC	CUT	TO YIELD
From *each* fat quarter	3—2" x 15" strips	Strip sets
Indigo print	3—2" x 40" strips	Vertical sashes, borders
	3—2" x 40" strips	Binding

Sew exact ¼" seams throughout. Place fabrics right sides together for sewing, unless otherwise noted.

Assemble the Strip Sets

(Make 6)

1. Sew together three different 2" x 15" print strips to make a strip set. Press the seams all one direction. Repeat for the remainder of the 2" x 15" strips.

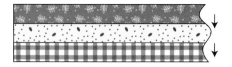

2. Cut each of the strip sets into seven 2" wide units. You will have 42 units.

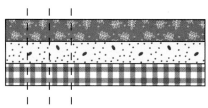

3. Sew 13 of these units together to form a strip, alternating the seams in each row. Press the seams all one direction. Make three rows of 13 units. You will have some units left over.

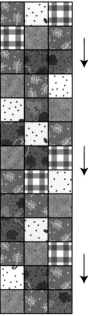

4. Measure, cut and sew the indigo sashing between the pieced rows from Step 3. Press toward the sashing.

Borders

Refer to page 10 for detailed instructions on adding borders.

1. Measure, cut and sew two borders the width of the quilt. Sew to the top and bottom of the quilt. Press toward the borders.

2. In the same manner, measure, cut and sew borders to the sides of the quilt. Press.

Quilting Suggestions

To prepare the quilt for quilting, layer the backing (which has been cut at least 4" larger than the quilt top) wrong side up, followed by the batting (again, cut larger than the quilt top) and last, the quilt top, right-side up. Thread or pin baste in a 4" grid across the quilt. Quilt as desired.

The quilt shown was hand quilted in a diagonal grid over the pieced rows. A simple cable was quilted in all of the sashes and borders with a cream-colored thread.

Binding

Refer to page 11 for detailed instructions on binding a quilt.

1. Before binding, hand baste a scant ¼" from the edge of the quilt to prevent the layers from shifting.

2. Join the binding strips with diagonal seams pressed open. Press the binding in half lengthwise with wrong sides together.

3. Sew the binding to the quilt with a ¼" seam. Trim excess batting and backing.

4. Turn the binding to the backside and stitch down by hand.

5. Sign and date your little quilt for the benefit of future quilt historians.

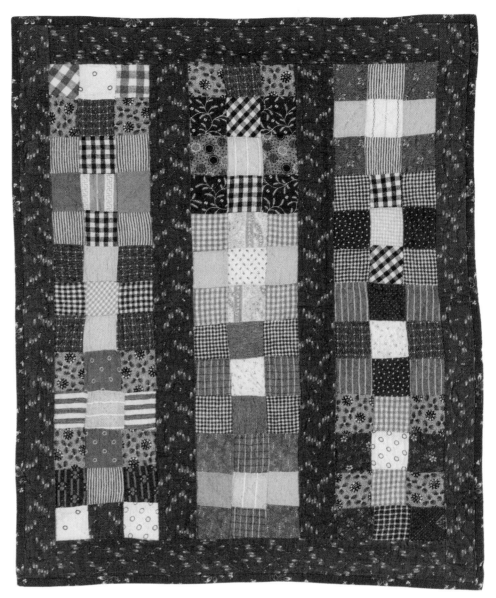

Cranberry Relish

Finished size: 16½" x 20½"
Block size: 3"

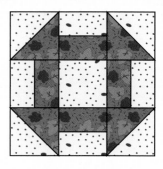

The various colors of red and pink in this quilt remind me of the colors of cranberry relish. You could choose your favorite color — just select six fabrics similar in color and hue, and one light fabric to make up this little quilt. This is basically a two-color quilt. Truly a quilt classic!

Fabric Requirements	Suggested Tool	Additional Supplies
Fat quarter background print	Easy Angle	Basic sewing supplies
Fat quarter of five red prints	*Note: If not using the Easy Angle,*	Thread to match fabric
Fat quarter (border)	*cut 24 squares 1⅞". Cut once on*	21" x 25" batting
⅝ yd. backing	*the diagonal to make triangles.*	

Cutting Directions

FABRIC	CUT	TO YIELD
Background	4—1½" x 20" strips	12—1½" squares
		48 Easy Angle triangles*
	Trim remainder of strip to 1"	6—1" cornerstones
	4—1" x 20" strips	Strip sets
From *each* of **four** red prints	1—1½" x 20" strip	12 Easy Angle triangles*
	1—1" x 20" strip	Strip sets
From *one* red print	7—1" x 20" strips	17—1" x 3½" sashes
		Inner border
	4—2" x 20" strips	Binding
Border print	4—3" x 20" strips	Outer border

* Note: Layer the 1½" background and print strips, with right sides together, and cut with the Easy Angle. They are now ready to chain-sew.

Sew exact ¼" seams throughout. Place fabrics right sides together for sewing, unless otherwise noted.

Assemble the Blocks
(Make 12)

1. Sew together all the triangle-squares. Press toward the darker fabric.

Make 48

2. Sew the 1" print and background strips together on the long edges to make strip sets. Make four strip sets. Press. Cut each strip set into 12 units 1½".

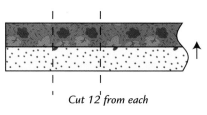

Cut 12 from each

3. Sew four triangle-squares, four matching strip-set units and one background square together to make a nine-patch block. Press as indicated.

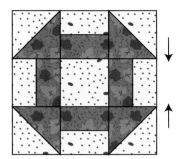

Make 12 blocks

Assemble the Quilt

1. Sew sashing strips between three blocks. Press toward the sashing.

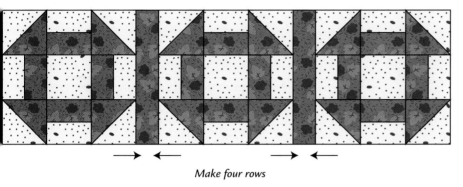

Make four rows

2. Sew three sashing strips and two cornerstones together to make a horizontal sashing row. Press toward the sashing.

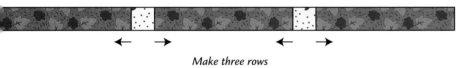

Make three rows

3. Sew the horizontal sashing rows between the block rows. Press toward the sashing.

Borders

Refer to page 10 for detailed instructions on adding borders.

1. Measure, cut and sew two narrow print borders to the top and bottom of the quilt. Press toward the borders. Repeat for the sides of the quilt.

2. In the same manner, measure, cut and sew wider print borders to the quilt. Press toward the borders.

Quilting Suggestions

To prepare the quilt for quilting, layer the backing (which has been cut at least 4" larger than the quilt top) wrong side up, followed by the batting (again, cut larger than the quilt top) and last, the quilt top, right-side up. Thread or pin baste in a 4" grid across the quilt. Quilt as desired.

The quilt shown was hand quilted in the ditch around each of the blocks, around the square in the center of each block and between the two borders. The lines of the leaves and ferns in the border were echoed by quilting.

Binding

Refer to page 11 for detailed instructions on binding a quilt.

1. Before binding, hand baste a scant ¼" from the edge of the quilt.

2. Join the binding strips with diagonal seams pressed open.

3. Press the binding strip in half lengthwise with wrong sides together.

4. Sew the double binding to the quilt with a ¼" seam. Trim excess batting and backing.

5. Turn the binding to the backside and stitch down by hand with matching thread.

6. Sign and date.

Peppermint Twist

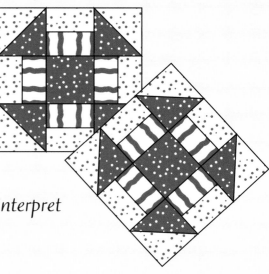

Finished size: 18" x 22"
Block size: 3"

The red and white stripe in this quilt reminds me of peppermint twist candies. This quilt is fun to make in bright reds and whites, but feel free to interpret it in any coloration.

Fabric Requirements

Fat quarter background print
½ yd. (or 2 fat quarters) red polka dot
½ yd. (or 2 fat quarters) red stripe
⅝ yd. backing

Suggested Tools

Easy Angle
Companion Angle
Note: If not using the Easy Angle, cut 1⅞" squares. Cut once on the diagonal for triangles.

Additional Supplies

Basic sewing supplies
Thread to match fabric
22" x 26" batting

Cutting Directions for Block A

FABRIC	CUT	TO YIELD
Background print	3—1½" x 20" strips	48 Easy Angle triangles*
	4—1" x 20" strips	Strip sets
Red polka dot	2—1½" x 40" strips	48 Easy Angle triangles*
		12—1½" squares
Red stripe	2—1" x 40" strips	4—1" x 20" strips (strip sets)

Note: Layer 1½" background and red polka dot strips, with right sides together, and cut with the Easy Angle. They are now ready to chain-sew.

Sew exact ¼" seams throughout. Place fabrics right sides together for sewing, unless otherwise noted.

Churn Dash Block Assembly (Make 12)

1. Sew together all the triangle-squares. Press toward the red triangle. Trim "dog-ears."

←

Make 48

2. Sew the long edges of the 1" red stripe and background print strips together, making four strip sets. Cut into 48 units 1½".

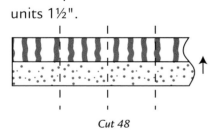

↑

Cut 48

3. Sew the strip-set units between the triangle-squares. Press.

→   ←

Make 24

4. Sew the red polka dot squares between two strip sets. Press.

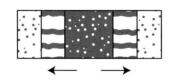

←   →

Make 12

5. Sew the Step 3 and 4 units together to make 12 blocks. At this point the blocks should measure 3½". Press.

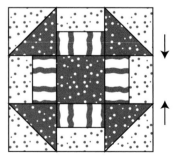

↓

↑

Make 12

Alternate Block Cutting Directions

FABRIC	CUT	TO YIELD
Background print	4—1¼" x 20" strips	12—1¼" x 3½" strips
		12—1¼" x 2" strips
Red polka dot	1—2" x 40" strip	6—2" squares

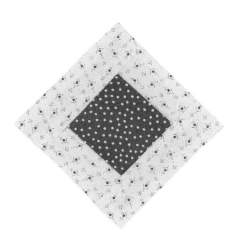

Alternate Block Assembly (Make 6)

1. Sew the 1¼" x 2" background rectangles to opposite sides of the red polka dot squares. Press.

2. Sew the 1¼" x 3½" background rectangles to the remaining sides of the Step 1 units. Press. At this point the alternate blocks should measure 3½".

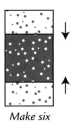

Make six

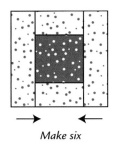

Make six

Cutting Directions for Setting Triangles and Borders

FABRIC	CUT	TO YIELD
Background print	1—2" x 20" strip	10—2" squares
Red polka dot	2—1½" x 40" strips	28 Companion Angle* triangles
	3—2½" x 40" strips	Outer border
Red stripe	3—1" x 40" strips	Inner border
	2" bias strips	Binding

Note: If not using the Companion Angle, cut seven 3¼" squares. Cut twice on the diagonal.

Setting Triangles Assembly

1. Sew red polka dot triangles to adjacent edges of the background print squares. Press.

2. Sew the remaining red polka dot triangles together on one short edge to make pairs. Press.

Make 10

Make four

Assemble the Quilt Top

1. Lay out the Churn Dash blocks, the alternate blocks and the pieced setting triangles in diagonal rows according to the photo on page 103.

2. Sew the blocks in each row together, pressing toward the alternate blocks and setting triangles.

3. Sew the rows together, pinning at each seam intersection. Press the rows all one direction. Add the corner triangles last.

4. Trim the edges straight if necessary, making certain to leave a ¼" seam allowance around the edge.

Borders

Refer to page 10 for detailed instructions on adding borders.

1. Measure and cut the narrow stripe borders the width of the quilt. Sew to the top and bottom of the quilt. Press toward the borders. Repeat for the sides of the quilt.

2. In the same manner, measure, cut and sew the red polka dot outer borders to the quilt. Press toward the red polka dot borders.

Quilting Suggestions

Mark any quilting designs. To prepare the quilt for quilting, layer the backing (which has been cut at least 4" larger than the quilt top) wrong side up, followed by the batting (again, cut larger than the quilt top) and last, the quilt top, right-side up. Thread or pin baste in a 4" grid across the quilt. Quilt as desired.

The quilt shown was machine stitched in the ditch between the blocks, around the red center of the alternate blocks and around the red triangles in the pieced border. A line of quilting was stitched on both sides of the narrow stripe border. A simple cable was hand quilted in the red polka dot border.

Binding

Refer to page 11 for detailed instructions on adding binding to a quilt.

1. Before binding, hand baste a scant ¼" from the edge of the quilt.

2. Join the bias binding strips with ¼" diagonal seams pressed open.

3. Fold the binding strip in half lengthwise with wrong sides together. Press.

4. Sew the binding to the quilt with a ¼" seam. Trim the excess batting and backing.

5. Turn the binding to the backside and stitch down by hand with matching thread.

6. Sign and date your little Peppermint Twist quilt!

Peppermint Drop

Finished size: 5" x 13½"
Block size: 3"

Leftover blocks? No problem....
Just put them together in this setting,
and in no time at all you'll have a small
quilt runner for a boutique table or a long
narrow quilt to hang in a special spot. So cute,
you may even make several!

Fabric Requirements

3½" x 20" (or fat quarter)
 background
6" x 20" (or fat quarter) red-white
 stripe
1½" x 20" (or fat quarter) small
 red polka dot
3" x 20" (or fat quarter) large red
 polka dot
1 fat quarter backing

Suggested Tools

Easy Angle
Companion Angle
*Note: If not using the Easy Angle,
cut 1⅞" squares. Cut once on the
diagonal to make triangles. If not using
the Companion Angle, cut one 5¾"
square. Cut twice on the diagonal to
make four triangles.*

Additional Supplies

Basic sewing supplies
Thread to match fabric
7" x 16" batting

Cutting Directions

FABRIC	CUT	TO YIELD
Background	1—1½" x 20" strip	12 Easy Angle triangles*
		3—1½" squares
	1—1" x 20" strip	Strip set
Red-white stripe	1—1½" x 20" strip	12 Easy Angle triangles*
	1—2¾" x 20" strip	4 Companion Angle triangles
Small red polka dot	1—1" x 20" strip	Strip set
Large red polka dot	2—1¼" x 20" strips	Binding

*Note: Layer the 1½" background and red-white stripe strips, with right sides together, and cut with the Easy Angle.
They are now ready to chain-sew.*

Sew exact ¼" seams throughout. Place fabrics right sides together for sewing, unless otherwise noted.

Assemble the Blocks (Make 3)

1. Assemble three blocks according to the directions on page 100.

2. Sew the Companion Angle triangles to the sides of the blocks as shown. Press

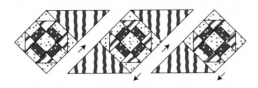

3. Sew the rows together. Press the seams toward the center.

Quilting Suggestions

To prepare the quilt for quilting, layer the backing (which has been cut at least 4" larger than the quilt top) wrong side up, followed by the batting (again, cut larger than the quilt top) and last, the quilt top, right-side up. Thread or pin baste in a 4" grid across the quilt. Quilt as desired.

The quilt shown was machine stitched in the ditch between the blocks and triangles and around the center square in the blocks.

Binding

Refer to page 11 for detailed instructions on binding a quilt.

1. Hand baste a scant ¼" from the edge of the quilt to prevent the layers from shifting while the binding is being sewn on.

2. Join the binding ends with ¼" diagonal seams pressed open. Sew to the quilt with a ¼" seam.

3. Turn the binding to the backside and turn under ¼". Stitch down by hand with matching thread.

4. Sign and date this cute little quilt.

Batik Baskets

Finished size: 18½" x 23"
Block size: 3"

Don't you just love the beautiful batiks available on the market today? The depth and motion achieved with the subtle color variations in the fabric are just incredible! This little quilt uses only three different fabrics; one light, and two complementary fabrics. Easy to make, yet visually dramatic!

Fabric Requirements

Fat quarter light blue batik background
½ yd. hot pink batik
Fat quarter dark purple batik
¾ yd. backing

Suggested Tools

Easy Angle
Companion Angle
Note: If not using the Easy Angle, cut 3⅞" and 1⅞" squares respectively. If not using the Companion Angle, cut three 6¼" squares. Cut twice on the diagonal.

Additional Supplies

Basic sewing supplies
Thread to match fabric
23" x 27" batting

Cutting Directions

FABRIC	CUT	TO YIELD
Light blue batik	1—3½" x 20" strip	2—3½" squares, cut once on the diagonal (corners). Trim remainder of strip to 3", cut four Companion Angle triangles
	1—3" x 20" strip	6 Companion Angle triangles
	6—1½" x 20" strips	108 Easy Angle triangles*
Hot pink batik	1—3½" x 40" strip	12 Easy Angle triangles
	1—1½" x 40" strip	36 Easy Angle triangles*
	3—3" x 40" strips	Border
Dark purple batik	1—3½" x 20" strip	6 Easy Angle triangles
	1—1½" x 20" strip	18 Easy Angle triangles*
	4—2" x 20" strips	Binding

Note: Layer background and hot pink 1½" strips with right sides together. Cut the Easy Angle triangles. They are now ready to chain-sew. Repeat with the 1½" dark purple strips. Cut 54 extra background triangles (for a total of 108 background triangles).

Sew exact ¼" seams throughout. Place fabrics right sides together for sewing, unless otherwise noted.

Assemble the Blocks
(Make 12 pink, 6 purple)

1. Sew together all the small triangle-squares. Press toward the darker fabric. Trim "dog-ears."

2. Assemble the top of the basket, adding the extra background triangles. Press as shown. Make 12 pink and six purple units.

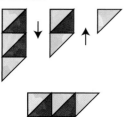

3. Sew the top of the basket units from Step 2 to the matching bottom of the baskets. Press toward the bottom of the basket.

Make 12 pink

Make six purple

Assemble the Quilt

1. Arrange the blocks in diagonal rows. Place the darker blocks in the center and the setting triangles along the edge. See the quilt photo for placement.

2. Sew the blocks and triangles together in rows. Press the seams in the rows all one direction, alternating the direction each row is pressed.

3. Sew the rows together, matching and pinning at seam intersections. Press the seams all one direction. Add the corner triangles last. Press.

Borders

Refer to page 10 for detailed instructions on adding borders.

1. Measure, cut and sew two hot pink borders the width of the quilt. Press toward the borders.

2. Repeat for the sides of the quilt. Press.

Quilting Suggestions

To prepare the quilt for quilting, layer the backing (which has been cut at least 4" larger than the quilt top) wrong side up, followed by the batting (again, cut larger than the quilt top) and last, the quilt top, right-side up. Thread or pin baste in a 4" grid across the quilt. Quilt as desired. The quilt shown was machine quilted in the ditch between each of the blocks, between the top and the bottom of the baskets, and between the quilt top and the borders.

Binding

Refer to page 11 for detailed instructions on binding a quilt.

1. Before binding, hand baste a scant ¼" from the edge of the quilt. This prevents the layers from shifting when the binding is being sewn on.

2. Join the binding strips with diagonal seams pressed open. Press the binding in half lengthwise with wrong sides together. Sew to the quilt with a ¼" seam allowance.

3. Trim excess batting and backing. Turn the binding to the backside and stitch down by hand with matching thread.

4. Sign and date your quilt!

Sailing Away!

Framed picture 9" x 15"

Do you need a quick and easy gift for a new baby? Would you like to decorate a nursery, but don't have the time or space for a wall quilt? This sweet framed set of blocks is the answer. All it takes is a purchased frame and the time to make up three easy blocks — no quilting necessary — and your project will be ready to hang!

Supplies

9" x 15" frame* with three 4" x 6" openings
Scraps of appropriate fabric for water, sky and boats
4" ribbon (color of your choice) 1" wide
Black embroidery floss

*Purchased at a discount store

Suggested Tool

Tri-Recs
Note: There is no substitute for the Tri-Recs tools.

Sew exact ¼" seams throughout. Place fabrics right sides together for sewing, unless otherwise noted.

Additional Supplies

Basic sewing supplies
Thread to match fabric
7" x 13" batting

Cutting Directions

Refer to page 122 for detailed instructions on using the Tri-Recs tool.

1. Using the information in the cutting diagram below, cut enough pieces for three blocks, varying the colors of the boats and sails.

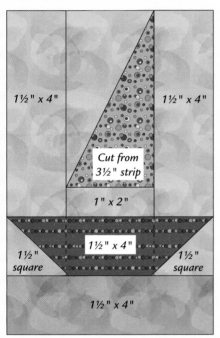

2. The sail and sky units are cut from 3½" wide strips with the Recs part of the Tri-Recs set of tools.

3. Place the two fabrics (sail and sky) both wrong sides up, and cut. With right sides together, and small ends opposite, sew together.

Assemble the Blocks (Make 3)

1. Sew all the sail and sky units. Press toward the sail. Add a sky rectangle to the bottom of the sail/sky unit and a long sky rectangle to the left side of the sails. Press. Cut a small triangle from ribbon. Insert it in the seam as you sew the long sky rectangle to the right side of the sail.

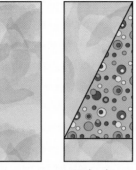

Make three

2. Crease or draw a diagonal line on the wrong side of the blue sky 1½" squares. Sew on opposite ends of the sailboat rectangle (A). Trim seams to ¼", and press seams toward the boat. Add a rectangle of water fabric beneath the boat (B).

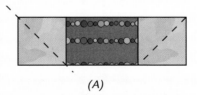

(A)

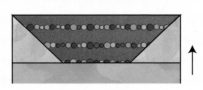

(B) Make three

3. Join the sky and sail units to the boat and water units. Press seams toward the boats. Make three blocks. At this point the blocks should measure 4" x 6".

4. With two strands of black embroidery floss, outline stitch in the vertical seam between the sail and the sky.

Frame the Blocks

1. Cut a piece of thin batting approximately 6½" x 12½". Layer the blocks and batting. Spray or hand baste a scant ¼" around the blocks, butting the blocks up to each other, but not overlapping.

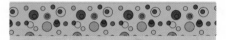

Note: Before basting, check to see how the blocks fit into your frame. You may need to adjust the space between the blocks.

2. Layer the picture frame backing wrong side up and the blocks with batting right-side up. Place the frame over the blocks. The backing should fit snugly, holding the blocks in place. It may be necessary to trim some excess batting to make the backing piece fit snugly.

3. Enjoy your framed quilt picture!

Hot Tamales!

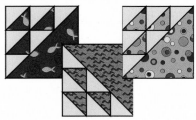

Finished size: 18" x 22"
Block size: 3"

Hot, bright colors in a zingy setting! Really simple Birds-in-Air blocks are given a spin, then set off with prairie points for a spicy finish. An easy quilt to make, but what a sizzling statement it makes!

Fabric Requirements

2 fat quarters (or ⅓ yd.) yellow
    mottled or solid
6 fat quarters of assorted
    bright prints
⅔ yd. backing

Suggested Tool

Easy Angle
Note: If not using the Easy Angle,
cut 3⅞" and 1⅞" squares,
respectively. Cut once on the
diagonal to make the triangles.

Additional Supplies

Basic sewing supplies
Thread to match fabric
22" x 26" batting

Cutting Directions

FABRIC	CUT	TO YIELD
Yellow mottled	10—1½" x 20" strips	180 Easy Angle triangles*
	4—1" x 20" strips	Borders
From *each* of the six bright prints	1—3½" x 20" strip	5—3½" Easy Angle triangles
	1—1½" x 20" strip	15 Easy Angle triangles*
	1—2½" x 20" strip	7—2½" squares (prairie points)

*Note: Layer the 1½" strips of yellow mottled fabric and the print strips, with right sides together, and cut Easy Angle triangles. They are now ready to chain-sew. (You will need to cut an additional 90 triangles from the yellow solid for a total of 180 triangles.)

Sew exact ¼" seams throughout. Place fabrics right sides together for sewing, unless otherwise noted.

Assemble the Blocks
(Make 30)

1. Sew together all the print and yellow triangle-squares. Press toward the print triangles. Trim "dog-ears."

Make 90

2. Sew together three identical triangle-squares and three additional yellow triangles to make this unit (A). Press the rows as indicated. When the unit (B) is complete, twist the seam where it intersects to open it. Press. Refer to page 10 for more instruction on this technique.

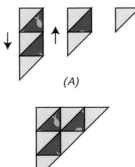

(A)

(B) Make 30

3. Join the pieced triangles to the matching large-print triangles. Press toward the large-print triangle. Trim "dog-ears." At this point the block should measure 3½".

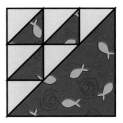

Make 30

4. Sew five blocks together in this manner. Press as indicated.

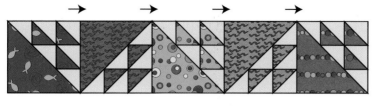

Make three rows

5. Sew five blocks together in this manner. Press as indicated.

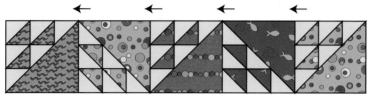

Make three rows

6. Join the rows, alternating Step 4 rows and Step 5 rows. Press the seams all in one direction.

Borders

Refer to page 10 for detailed instructions on adding borders.
1. Trim two narrow yellow borders the width of the quilt. Sew to the top and bottom of the quilt. Press toward the borders.

2. Repeat this procedure for the sides of the quilt.

Prairie Points

1. Fold each of the 2½" print squares in half once on the diagonal. Press. Fold again on the diagonal. Press.

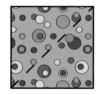 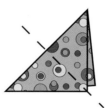 

Make 42

2. Baste nine prairie points together for the top and bottom of the quilt. Adjust as needed so the points on the prairie points come right to the corners of the quilt top. With points facing in, sew in place with a ¼" seam.

3. Repeat this procedure for the sides of the quilt, using 11 prairie points on each side. You will have two left over.

Quilting Suggestions

To prepare the quilt for quilting, layer the backing (which has been cut at least 4" larger than the quilt top) wrong side up, followed by the batting (again, cut larger than the quilt top) and last, the quilt top, right-side up. Thread or pin baste in a 4" grid across the quilt. Quilt as desired, **but leave the last inch around the edge of the quilt unquilted for now.** The quilt shown was quilted in the ditch between each block and on the diagonal lines created by the large triangles.

Finish the Quilt

1. To finish the edge, trim the batting and backing even with the raw edge of the quilt top.

2. Trim the batting ¼" shorter to reduce bulk.

3. Turn the prairie points to the outside of the quilt.

4. Turn the backing under ¼" and slip stitch the backing over the stitching line for the prairie points.

5. Finish any quilting around the edge of the quilt.

6. Sign and date the quilt.

Under the Sea

Finished size: 25¾" square
Block size: 5"

This small quilt looks difficult, but it isn't. It's the traditional Pineapple block constructed in a new, easy way. The choice of two different batik fabrics not only makes the fabric choices simpler, but also creates motion and depth through the color variation in the fabric. I named it Under the Sea because it has the illusion of water.

Fabric Requirements	**Suggested Tool**	**Additional Supplies**
1 yd. blue batik	Companion Angle	Basic sewing supplies
1 yd. green batik	*Note: If not using the Companion Angle, cut two 8¼" squares. Cut twice on the diagonal.*	Thread to match fabric
⅞ yd. backing		30" x 30" batting

Cutting Directions

FABRIC	CUT	TO YIELD
Blue batik	1—2½" x 40" strip	4—2½" squares (centers)
	4—2" x 40" strips	72—2" squares
	2—1½" x 40" strips	36—1½" squares
	4—1¼" x 40" strips	8—1¼" x 5½" rectangles
		16—1¼ " x 4" rectangles
		8—1¼" x 2½" rectangles
	4—2½" x 40" strips	Borders
Green batik	1—2½" x 40" strip	9—2½" squares (centers)
	2—2" x 40" strips	32—2" squares
	1—1½" x 40" strip	16—1½" squares
	8—1¼" x 40" strips	18—1¼" x 5½" rectangles
		36—1¼" x 4" rectangles
		18—1¼" x 2½" rectangles
	1—4" x 40" strip	8 Companion Angle triangles
	1—5" x 40" strip	2—5" squares, cut once on the diagonal (corner triangles)
	3— 2" x 40" strips	Binding

Sew exact ¼" seams throughout. Place fabrics right sides together for sewing, unless otherwise noted.

Piece the Blocks
(Make 9 Green, 4 Blue)

1. Mark a diagonal line on the wrong side of the blue 1½" squares (A). Place a blue 1½" square on one corner of a 2½" green square. Sew on the diagonal line. Press. Trim the seam to ¼". Repeat on all four corners. At this point the unit should measure 2½" square (B).

(A)   *(B) Make nine*

TIP: Instead of marking the sewing line, you can gently crease the square on the diagonal.

2. Sew 1¼" x 2½" green rectangles to opposite sides of the pieced center squares. Press toward the rectangles.

Make nine

3. Sew 1¼" x 4" green rectangles to the remaining two sides of the unit from Step 2. Press toward the rectangles. At this point the unit should measure 4" square.

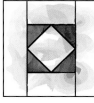

Make nine

4. Crease or mark a diagonal line on the 2" blue squares. Sew to each corner of the units from Step 3. Trim the seam to ¼" and press toward the triangles. At this point the unit should measure 4" square.

Make nine

5. Sew 1¼" x 4" green rectangles to opposite sides of the Step 4 units. Press toward the rectangles. Sew 1¼" x 5½" green rectangles to the remaining two sides of the unit. Press toward the rectangles. At this point the unit should measure 5½" square.

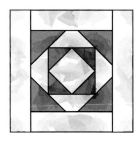

Make nine

6. Sew 2" blue squares to all four corners of the Step 5 units. Trim the seam to ¼", and press toward the triangles. At this point the blocks should measure 5½" square.

Make nine

7. Using the blue 2½" squares and the green 1½" squares, piece four centers, following the instructions in Step 1.

Make four

8. Using the blue rectangles and the green 2" squares, piece four blocks following Steps 2 through 6. Press the last four green corners toward the center of the block. At this point the blocks should measure 5½" square.

Make four

Assemble the Quilt

1. Arrange the blocks in diagonal rows, alternating the green and blue blocks as shown in the photo on page 119. Position the setting triangles along the edge. Note the setting triangles are slightly larger than needed. Place the smaller triangles on the corners.

2. Matching and pinning intersections, sew the blocks and triangles together in rows. Press the seams in alternating directions.

3. Matching and pinning seam intersections, sew the rows together, pressing the seams all one direction.

4. Trim the quilt top square, leaving at least a ¼" seam allowance around the outside edge.

Borders

Refer to page 10 for detailed instructions on adding borders.

1. Measure and cut two borders the width of the quilt. Sew to opposite sides of the quilt, pressing the seam towards the borders.

2. Measure and cut two borders the length of the quilt. Sew to the remaining two sides of the quilt, pressing the seams towards the borders.

Quilting Suggestions

To prepare the quilt for quilting, layer the backing (which has been cut at least 4" larger than the quilt top) wrong side up, followed by the batting (again, cut larger than the quilt top)

and last, the quilt top, right-side up. Thread or pin baste in a 4" grid across the quilt. Quilt as desired. The quilt shown was machine quilted in the ditch between the blocks with invisible thread. Random loops were machine quilted in the setting triangles, and alternating stacked rows were quilted in the border with variegated thread.

Binding

Refer to page 11 for detailed instructions on binding a quilt.

1. Before binding, hand baste a scant ¼" from the edge of the quilt. This will keep the layers together and prevent shifting while the binding is being sewn on.

2. Join the binding strips with diagonal seams pressed open. Press the binding in half lengthwise with wrong sides together.

3. Sew to the quilt with a ¼" seam. Trim excess batting and backing.

4. Turn the binding to the backside and stitch down by hand with matching thread.

5. Sign and date your little quilt.

Tool Tutorial

Tri-Recs™ Tools

To cut Tri triangles, lay the tool on the strip with the top flat edge at the top of the strip, and a line on the tool aligned with the bottom of the strip. Cut on both sides of the triangle. The patterns will tell you what size strip to cut — always ½" larger than the finished size.

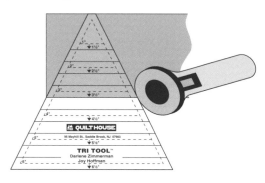

For the second cut, rotate the tool so it is pointing down. Align as before and cut.

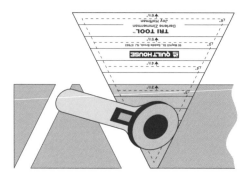

To cut Recs triangles, cut the same size strip as for the large triangles. Leave the strip folded and you will automatically cut pairs of Recs triangles. Align the tool with the flat top edge

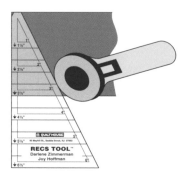

at the top of the strip, and a line on the tool aligned with the bottom of the strip. Cut on the angled edge, then swing around and nip off the "magic angle" at the top. This needs to be cut accurately, as it is your alignment guide when sewing the pieces together.

For the second cut, rotate the tool so it is pointing down. Align as before and cut, then swing back and trim off the "magic angle."

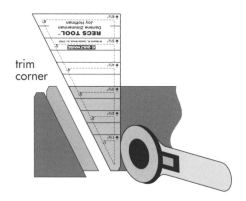

trim corner

Together the two tools cut the shapes for making a triangle within a square. Lay out the pieces as shown to form a square.

Fit the Recs triangle into the corner of the large triangle. Note how the "magic angle" will fit right into the corner as shown. Yes, the pieces look odd at this point, but they will be right when sewn!

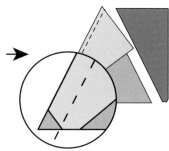

Triangle Tables for Tri-Recs

Use these triangle tables to determine the number of Tri or Recs triangles you can cut from a 42" strip of fabric.

Tri tool

Finished Size	Strip Width	Number of Triangles
1"	1½"	38
1½"	2"	31
2"	2½"	25
2½"	3"	21
3"	3½"	19
3½"	4"	17
4"	4½"	15
4½"	5"	13
5"	5½"	12
5½"	6"	11
6"	6½"	10

Recs tool

Finished Size	Strip Width	Number of Triangles
1"	1½"	52
1½"	2"	44
2"	2½"	40
2½"	3"	34
3"	3½"	32
3½"	4"	28
4"	4½"	24
4½"	5"	24
5"	5½"	22
5½"	6"	22
6"	6½"	20

Easy Angle™

This tool comes in two different sizes, 4½" and 6½". You may use either one for the projects in this book. Easy Angle allows you to cut triangle squares from the same size strip as for squares. You only need to add a ½" seam allowance when using Easy Angle (instead of that nasty ⅞" you add when cutting squares, then cutting on the diagonal).

To use the tool most efficiently, layer the fabric strips you are using for your triangle squares right sides together, then cut with Easy Angle. They will then be ready to chain-sew.

Before making the first cut, trim off the selvages. Then align the top flat edge of the tool at the top of the strip, matching a line on the tool with the bottom edge of the strip. Cut on the diagonal edge.

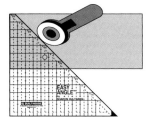

To make the second cut, rotate the tool so the flat edge is aligned at the bottom of the strip, and a line on the tool is aligned with the top of the strip. Cut again.

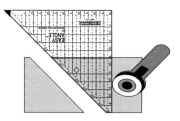

Continue in this manner down the strip. Chain-sew the triangles on the longest edge. Press toward the darkest fabric and trim "dog-ears."

Note: If you choose not to use Easy Angle in the projects, you will need to add ⅞" to the finished sizes of the triangle squares. Then cut a strip that width.

For example, instead of cutting a 2½" strip to yield 2" triangle squares, cut a 2⅞" strip instead. Then cut squares, and cut the squares once on the diagonal.

Companion Angle™

Companion Angle allows you to cut quarter-square triangles — or triangles with the longest edge on the straight-of-grain. A common use for this type of triangle is the "goose" in flying geese.

To cut with Companion Angle, align the top flat point of the tool with the top edge of the strip. A line on the tool should align with the bottom of the strip. Cut on both sides of the tool.

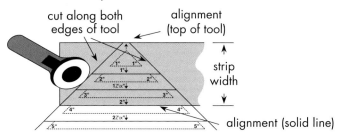

For the next cut, rotate the tool so the point of the tool is at the bottom of the strip, and a line on the tool is aligned with the bottom of the strip. Cut again. Continue in this manner down the strip of fabric.

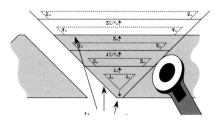

Note: If not using the Companion Angle, you will need to add 1¼" to the finished size of the base of the triangle you are cutting. Cut a square that size, then cut it twice on the diagonal to yield 4 triangles. For example, the "goose" you are cutting will finish to 3" across the base. Add 1¼" + 3" = 4¼". Cut a 4¼" square, then cut twice to yield 4 triangles.

Triangle Tables for Easy Angle™

Finished Size of Triangle	From	Number from Strip
½" triangles	1" strip	50
1" triangles	1½" strip	38
1½" triangles	2" strip	30
2" triangles	2½" strip	26
2½" triangles	3" strip	22
3" triangles	3½" strip	20
3½" triangles	4" strip	18
4" triangles	4½" strip	16
4½" triangles	5" strip	14
5" triangles	5½" strip	12
5½" triangles	6" strip	12
6" triangles	6½" strip	12

Triangle Tables for Companion Angle™

Finished Base of Triangle	From	Number from Strip
1" triangles	1" strip	34
2" triangles	1½" strip	23
3" triangles	2" strip	17
4" triangles	2½" strip	13
5" triangles	3" strip	12
6" triangles	3½" strip	9
7" triangles	4" strip	8
8" triangles	4½" strip	7
9" triangles	5" strip	7
10" triangles	5½" strip	5

Easy Scallop™

Assembling:

The scallop tools need to be assembled before using. Bend up the tabs located at the bottom of the tools. Insert the tabs through the hole in the matching piece, being careful to keep the printed side up on each of the pieces. Once the tabs are inserted, flatten the tabs and the tool is ready to use. You have two different size tools ranging in size from 4" to 12".

Measuring:

Measure the length of the border. Choose the desired number of scallops. Divide the border length by that number to yield the scallop size. Round the answer to the nearest quarter inch. Set the Easy Scallop tool at that size. EX: 72" border divided by 7 scallops = 10.285". Round to 10¼". Set the tool at 10¼".

Marking:

To mark a rounded corner, begin at the very corner of the quilt and mark a full scallop. Mark from both ends toward the center and adjust the center scallop as needed. When you mark the adjacent edge with a full scallop, the corner will automatically be rounded.

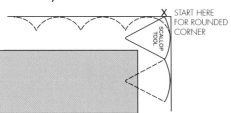

To mark a pointed corner or "ears," begin at one corner with a half scallop. Again, mark from both ends to the center, adjusting the center scallop as needed. As you mark the adjacent side with a half scallop, the "ear" will be formed.

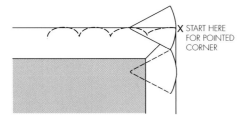

Binding

Do not cut on the marked line! Quilt, then before binding, hand-baste along the marked line to keep the layers from shifting when the binding is attached.

A bias binding is a must for binding curved edges. Cut a 1¼" single-bias binding. (Refer to page 11 for detailed instructions on preparing binding.)

1. With raw edges of binding aligned with the marked line on your quilt, begin sewing a ¼" seam. Stitch to the base of the "V", stop with the needle down and lift the presser foot.

2. Pivot the quilt and binding around the needle. Put the presser foot down and begin stitching out of the "V", taking care not to stitch any pleats into the binding.

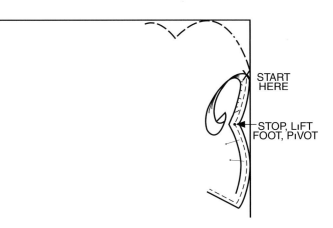

3. Continue around the quilt in this manner, easing the binding around the curves and pivoting at the inside of the "V".

4. Trim the seam allowance an even ¼", turn to the backside and stitch down by hand with matching thread, covering the stitching line. At the "V", the binding will just fold over upon itself making a little pleat.

Tools

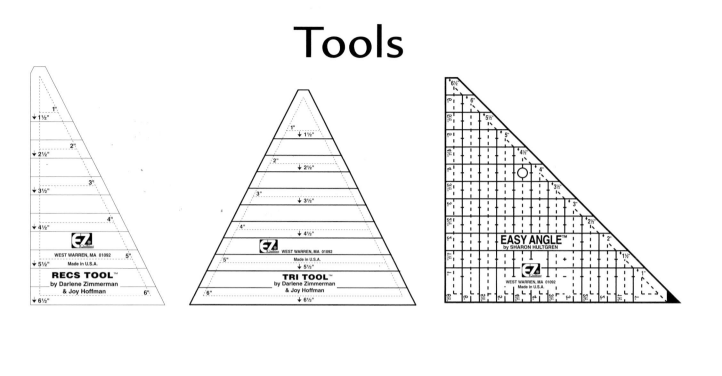

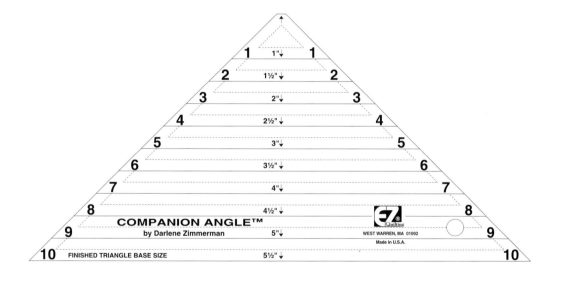

All these tools can be found at your local quilt, craft or fabric store. If you cannot find the EZ tools locally, you can call (800) 660-0415 to order from EZ Quilting by Wrights.

Resources

American and Efird Inc.

(A & E Threads)

P.O. Box 507

Mt. Holly, NC 28120

(708) 822-6014

http://www.amefird.com

Chanteclaire Fabrics

11 E. 36th St.

New York, NY 10016

(212) 686-5194

http://www.chanteclairefabrics.com

EZ Quilting by Wrights

85 South St.

P.O. Box 398

West Warren, MA 01092

(800) 660-0415

http://www.ezquilt.com

Easy Scallop

Easy Angle

Companion Angle

Tri-Recs

Fairfield Processing Corp.

P.O. Box 1157

Danbury, CT 06813-1157

(800) 980-8000

http://www.poly-fil.com

Hobbs Bonded Fibers

P.O. Box 2521

Waco, TX 76702-2521

(800) 433-3357

http://www.hobbsbondedfibers.com

Thermore batting

RJR Fabrics

2203 Dominguez Street

Building K-3

Torrance, CA 90501

(800) 422-5426

Info@rjrfabrics.com

http://www.rjrfabrics.com

Roxanne International

Roxanne's Glue Baste-It

Sold at your local quilt shop.

Adam Beadworks

P.O. Box 2476

Guerneville, CA 95446

(707) 869-2556

http://www.threadheaven.com

Thread Heaven

Badger Basket Company

P.O. Box 227

Edgar, WI 54426-0227

(800) 236-1310

kp@badgerbasket.com

http://www.badgerbasket.com

Moses basket

Lorie's Little Quilts

241 Country Road 120

Carthage, MO 64836

(888) 419-5618

lorie@lorie'slittlequilts.com

Quilt hangers